Clippings

All of the Other Cool Stuff That Didn't Fit Into the First Book

ANDREW LINKER

DEDICATION

To the ballplayers, managers and coaches who over my career always
filled my notebooks with something interesting to share.

And in memory of Larry O'Rourke, an outstanding writer and an even
better friend who faced death far better than most of us handle life.

TABLE OF CONTENTS

Clippings

All of the Other Cool Stuff That
Didn't Fit Into the First Book

Introduction

The baseball clubhouse once was the ultimate sanctuary, the place where players, coaches and managers truly could roam the room with nary an inhibition.

This was a place where anything could be said to anybody at any time with little chance of anyone outside its walls ever knowing what was being said or done.

This was a place where no one was ever truly surprised to see teammates – dragging from their debauchery of the night before – quietly drinking coffee by the urn or popping amphetamines as if they were so many M&Ms.

This was – and still is – a place that often has been its own United Nations, a place shared by whites, blacks, Latinos, Asians and an occasional Aussie whose only common characteristics are playing a game better than nearly everyone else on the planet, earning millions of dollars for playing that game and, well, belching.

Ballplayers, like so many of us, enjoy a good burp. Most of us try to do so quietly. Not ballplayers. For many of them, belching can become an art form. They relish in burping louder and longer than any of their teammates, and they do so with impunity inside the walls of the alpha male clubhouse.

For generations, the clubhouse has been the ultimate frat house, where the party is interrupted only by something as banal as a ballgame that needed to be played.

"We used to have a lot of fun in the clubhouse," Hall of Fame second baseman Bill Mazeroski once said of the Pirates' old digs at Pittsburgh's already-ancient Forbes Field.

"Did you know," Mazeroski said, "we used to sing all the time?"

Sing? Like songs?

"Yes. Country songs. We all liked them."

Everybody?

"Yes."

Even the Great Clemente?

"Oh, yes," Mazeroski said, "even Clemente."

Of course, this was back in the 1950s and '60s, when such activities – who knew Roberto Clemente, the greatest player ever to emerge from Puerto Rico, could belt out a little Tex Ritter? – rarely were chronicled by the attending media.

Back then, the term "sports journalism" was an oxymoron.

That all changed shortly after Mazeroski retired as a player in 1972 – right around the time the nation was first learning of a break-in at an office complex in the Foggy Bottom neighborhood of Washington, D.C.

The 1972 burglary at the Watergate eventually brought down the White House, leading to Richard Nixon's resignation in 1974 and spawning a generation of journalists who wanted to be the next Bob Woodward and Carl Bernstein – the two dogged reporters responsible for helping bring down Tricky Dick and his corrupt administration.

The new age of journalism brought with it not only a revamped look at how the media covered the news but also in how the media viewed the sporting world and the athletes they once shielded.

While Jim Bouton's 1970 groundbreaking book *Ball Four* shocked baseball's mostly staid establishment by exposing the shenanigans of the clubhouse, the post-Watergate media pushed for more than what could be found in black-and-white boxscores.

After *Ball Four* and Watergate, the media – already a fixture, albeit a mostly benign one, inside the clubhouse – became more aggressive and soon became weeds in what was once the ballplayers' Eden.

"They're vultures, all vultures," former major league catcher Rick Sweet said of modern-day sports writers whose careers have been built on watching and reporting everything they see. The operative word here being "everything."

Sweet said he once found a sports writer hiding in a bathroom stall inside the clubhouse at New York's Shea Stadium – apparently wanting to listen in on some conversations, although no one knew for sure just how much inside poop that writer picked up from listening to players take, well, an inside poop.

Sweet, a baseball lifer, has mellowed over his career, which started as a player in 1975 and continued as a minor league manager well into the new millennium.

Sweet is a real-life version of Crash Davis, the fictional catcher in the movie "Bull Durham" who depending on the scene could be either the story's protagonist or antagonist.

Sweet, like Kevin Costner's Crash Davis, is part-optimist, part-cynic, part-humorist, part-philosopher. He is full-time wise to the ways of baseball, knowing that the game can be a microcosm of life in the real world.

He knows nobody is perfect, that errors are made. Somebody wins, somebody loses. And then you do it all over the next day.

"Everything in baseball is written in pencil," Sweet would say often in his season-plus as the Class AA Harrisburg Senators' manager during the 1998 and '99 seasons.

"And everything," Sweet said, "is written with a big eraser."

Only one problem there. Sports writers today rarely use erasers. They scribble down everything onto notepads and into iPads, eventually recycling that information into game stories, features, columns and, thanks to the advent of the Internet, those ubiquitous blogs and tweets.

Nearly everything is kept, from scraps of paper to old, yellowed newspaper clips to even older, more yellowed boxscores of games long forgotten by their participants. With the Internet – thank you, Al Gore – everything today, from feat to faux pas, is only a couple of mouse clicks away, having already been preserved for posterity in cyberspace.

The 2012 book *One Patch of Grass* took a peek into the sacred clubhouse on Harrisburg's historic City Island and into the lives of the Hall of Famers, all-stars, no-stars, wanna-bes and never-weres who since 1890 have summered on a 63-acre parcel of land in the middle of Pennsylvania's Susquehanna River.

One Patch of Grass examined the astounding, if relatively anonymous, life of Spottswood Poles, the wonderfully talented, Hall of Fame-caliber outfielder who had been born black in an era when only whites were allowed to play in the major leagues.

There also were stories of the magnificent Vladimir Guerrero, Ryan Zimmerman and Stephen Strasburg – three uber-prospects who fast-tracked their way to the major leagues – as well as tales on the Sisyphean struggles of Curtis Pride and Jamey Carroll to not only reach the majors but to stay there for more than a decade.

Clippings isn't like that.

Mostly because this a book devoid of, well, stories.

Clippings is a companion piece for *One Patch of Grass*, a chance to augment the free-flowing history presented in that book with notes, quotes and an occasional anecdote that could not be squeezed into the first book. Basically, it's a slice of cold pizza in the morning and, really, who doesn't like a slice of cold pizza in the morning?

Harrisburg has been blessed over the years to have ballplayers, managers and coaches who have been conversational, controversial and crusty.

Sometimes all at once.

Dave Trembley, the Senators' first manager during their rebirth in 1987, saw himself as a teacher both for the players and the fans, educating the former on how to play the game and the latter on how to watch it.

Jim Tracy, the incarnation of Norman Vincent Peale with a fungo bat during his lone season managing the 100-win Senators in 1993, was just as likely to talk about family and fishing as he was about hitting and pitching.

Then there was Doug Sisson, the manager of Harrisburg's 1999 championship team who was a writer's best friend by filling notepads with unfiltered thoughts, unwavering opinions and an occasional unworldly rant or two.

Really, who else can get himself hired for a job that he would quit in a huff, lobby hard to win back the same job a week later and then be summarily fired from the same job that he had so badly wanted, quit and then wanted again? All within 22 months.

Sisson's lengthy list of deeds and d'ohs over his season-plus on City Island filled enough notepads to take up two Hammermill paper boxes.

His words earned their own chapter in this book.

Then there have been the players – past and present – who would share their thoughts on everything from being chased by autograph hounds to being tempted by performance-enhancing drugs to being able to stretch their last dollar on a meager minor league salary that makes flipping pizzas back home look like an upward career move.

Their thoughts really are no different today than those of players back in Bill Mazeroski's days or in 1987 when Dave Trembley's Senators returned to City Island after a 35-year hiatus.

Some of the musings in *Clippings* may make you laugh.

Others may make you cringe, especially when you learn just how little minor leaguers are paid compared to their major league brethren.

There are thoughts that go beyond the game – from onetime pitching prospect Joey Eischen talking of quitting baseball and spending more time with his family to career minor leaguer Hassan Pena talking about fleeing Cuba for America not to play a boys' game but to live a life free of one man's tyranny.

Hopefully, all of the thoughts in *Clippings* – from the profound to the profane – will make you think about the lives of the men who play and coach the game, as well as how their outlooks on life may not be all that different from your own.

Andrew Linker
October 2013

Senators manager Dave Trembley, left, signs autographs along the third-base line on City Island in 1989 along with right fielder and Eastern League MVP Wes Chamberlain, pitcher Mouse Adams and infielder Tommy Shields

Autographs

"Hey, mister, sign my baseball"

Manager **Dave Trembley** (1987-89) on giving players advice to practice their penmanship:

    "I told them to sign their names so fans could read it, not write like they were a doctor or lawyer."

"It's an honor to sign autographs. It means I'm doing well enough that people want my autograph. If you don't do well, nobody wants your autograph, nobody cares about you."

Pitcher Gabe White
Class of '93

"In the minors, you might have 15 people waiting with one card or a piece of paper to sign. Then you get to the big leagues and it's worse. When you sign one autograph up there, you have to sign 100. Then you try to drive away at the ballpark and you have to roll down your window to sign, because they won't let you by unless you want to run them over."

First baseman-outfielder **Cliff Floyd** (1993)

Infielder **Jamey Carroll** (1998-2000, 2002) on joining Don Mattingly, Scott Rolen, George Foster and Hall of Famer Harmon Killebrew in 2004 to raise more than $100,000 to benefit youth programs in Carroll's hometown of Evansville, Indiana:

"To be on a stage with George Foster, Harmon Killebrew and Don Mattingly just opened my eyes. ... I drew a picture of Donnie just so he could sign it for me."

"If somebody wants my autograph, I feel honored. I'm not big celebrity guy. It gives you a chance to relate to the fans a little."

First baseman **Tyler Moore** (2011)

Baseball Cards

"Every once in a while you see yourself ..."

"I could open a set now and find over 100 players that I know from playing with or against them."

Infielder-coach **Greg Fulton** (1991-93)

Doug Piatt checks out his own cards in 1992

"It's really strange to go out and buy a pack of Topps cards like I used to, and my card might be in there."

Pitcher **Doug Piatt** (1992)

"You walk into a hobby store and see the Cal Ripkens and the Nolan Ryans on the box, and you'd like to see yourself there one day. Every once in a while you see yourself in a minor league set, but that's different."

Pitcher **Travis Buckley** (1992)

"Whatever you're in the game for, money or whatever, it's the ultimate to get a major league baseball card. A lot of guys never get those cards."

Pitching coach **Mike Parrott** (1992)

"Having a baseball card is what you dream about when you're a kid. It's one of those little things that mean a lot to a player."

Hitting coach **Rob Ducey** (2004)

TOPPS
CHEWING GUM
INCORPORATED

254-36th Street, Brooklyn, New York 11232
Telephone: (212) 768-8900, TWX: (710) 584-5488
Plant: Duryea, Pennsylvania

Agreement between:

_____JAMES EDWIN TRACY_____Player, and

TOPPS CHEWING GUM, INC.

We, the undersigned, hereby agree to extend the term of our
present contract, plus extensions, if any, for an additional
peroid of two years or two full Baseball Seasons, as the case
may be, on the same terms and conditions contained in said
contract. This extension agreement shall be governed by the
Laws of the State of New York.

A bonus payment of $75.00 will be due the player the first
time after signing this extension that he is or becomes an
active member of a Major League Baseball Team between May 15
and August 15.

x _____ x __5/29/81__
           PLAYER   DATE

TOPPS CHEWING GUM, INC.

_____ ___5-29-81__

Jim Tracy's 1981 contract with Topps to produce baseball cards of the then-
Chicago Cubs outfielder. Alas, baseball's work stoppage during the 1981 season
helped cut short the playing career of the man who 12 years later would manage
one of the greatest teams in the century-plus history of minor league baseball.

Career Paths

"I'm married to this game"

"I wouldn't have minded being a ballplayer. I played sandlot ball. I caught and played third. I wasn't too hot as a player, but I was a great bench jockey. I'm not kidding. I was very good at that."

Senators owner **Jerry Mileur** (1987-95)

"My job doesn't have a set pattern and that's what I like about it. One minute I'm sitting in a business meeting possibly discussing a contract and the next minute I may be unloading a box off a truck."

General manager **Rick Redd** (1987-92)

Scott Ruskin (1988-89) on switching from playing the outfield in the minors for a chance to pitch in the majors:

"I was going to be 25. I wasn't real thrilled about going back to Class A ball. I really didn't put up any numbers to convince myself that I would play outfield in this organization."

"The only way to get it done in baseball is to make it your life. I'm single, but I'm married to this game."

Manager **Mike Quade** (1991-92)

"I was a better hockey player than a baseball player. Hockey had always been my No. 1 sport. I've had people tell me they wished I had stayed in hockey. ... There were a few chances to go with Junior A teams in Ontario, but that was at the same time I got the chance to sign a pro baseball contract. The decision was easy. Baseball is more money, and it's warmer."

Utility player **Matt Stairs** (1991)

JOEY EISCHEN

"If I had an education, I might have retired and taken over a high school program. But my education is out here on the field, so I'm going to coach when I'm done playing. That's my plan. Hopefully, I'll be on the diamond until I croak."

Pitcher **Joey Eischen** (1993)

"**S**occer was my best sport, but there was no future in playing it."
Outfielder **Curtis Pride** (1993)

CURTIS PRIDE

Manager **Pat Kelly** (1995-96) on being 17 years old in 1973 and deciding on whether to sign with the California Angels or accept an appointment to the United States Naval Academy:

"Both my parents said, 'Whatever you decide is great.' And I'm thinking, 'No. You've told me what to do my whole life. Now, tell me

Infielder **Geoff Blum** (1996, 1998) on returning to Class AA in 1998, a move that ultimately jumpstarts Blum to a 14-year career in the majors:
"I was seriously debating if that was going to be the last call. You always want to progress; you never want to regress – and going back (in 1998 to Harrisburg) definitely felt more like a regression than a progression for me. That was the hardest part for me to swallow."

Manager **Rick Sweet** (1998-99) on briefly leaving the game in 2000:
"Somebody wants me as a substitute teacher for high school. I can do that. I can take over a classroom. You know, I can dominate a classroom."

Outfielder **Kenny James** (1999-2001) on turning down a college football scholarship at South Carolina in 1995 to sign with the Expos:
"Being a running back, I was going to get the ball 30, 35 times a game. Guys are trying, literally, to go out there and hurt you. I thought my body would last longer in baseball. And baseball is more of an individual sport than football. In football, you have to depend on the line to block for you. In baseball, if you get a good jump, you get the ball."

"I'm 51 years old and still putting on a baseball uniform, which is something I was doing at 6. I didn't think it would go on this long or that it would still be this much fun. Was there more to (being a pitching coach) than I thought there would be? Sure. I knew the general outline. I just didn't know how the paragraphs would fit."

Pitching coach **Jerry Reuss** (2000)

Pitching coach **Tommy John** (2002) on looking for a coaching job before the 2002 season:

"Most clubs don't want to disrupt the flow of coaches who have been in their organization, going through the system. The Expos were the best system for me because they didn't have any coaches."

"Even if I had been a big league pitcher for 10 years, I still would have wanted to punt for Texas A&M when I was done playing. And if punting doesn't work out, I'll go out and play intramural Wiffle Ball and lead the league in home runs."

Pitcher **Mark Mangum** (2001-02) on retiring at age 23

"I didn't leave Cuba because of baseball. I left Cuba because I wanted to be free."

Pitcher Hassan Pena (2010-11)

Manager **Keith Bodie** (2005) on the time between being fired by Houston in 2004 and being hired by Washington to manage Harrisburg in 2005:

"I was having a tough time finding a job. I felt like Ebenezer Scrooge in 'A Christmas Carol.' I was given a look at the past, present and future. I was given a great perspective of things. You find out what you can and can't do. I was faced with the very serious prospect of being out of the game. We were talking about starting a family business, but that was still in the research stage. That could have been anything from pushing lawnmowers to pushing hamburgers."

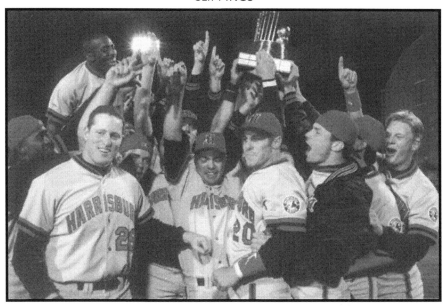

The Senators of '96 celebrate in Portland, Maine, after winning the first of their record four straight Eastern League titles. Among those celebrating are future major leaguers Vladimir Guerrero, top left; Jose Vidro and Brad Fullmer (20) center; and Geoff Blum, far right.

Championships

Harrisburg mayor **Stephen Reed** in 1987 after the Senators' championship in their first season back in baseball since 1952: "Were you to write a script for fiction, you couldn't write one any better than how the Senators' season unfolded."

Manager **Rick Sweet** (1998-99) after the Senators' third straight Eastern League title in 1998:

"When you taste this once, you want to taste it again and again. People who have never won never know this feeling."

The Senators' 1987 championship ring

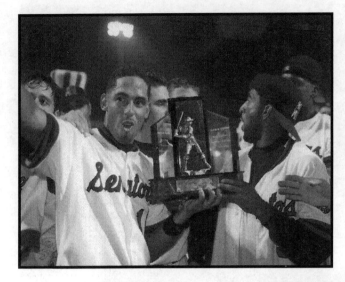

Hiram Bocachica, left, and Trovin Valdez show off some of the Eastern League's playoff hardware after the Senators win their second straight title in 1997, again beating Portland in the finals but this time on City Island

The Senators' three-peat, with pitcher Scott Forster (center) holding up the Eastern League trophy, comes in 1998 at New Britain, Conn.

The Senators celebrate an unprecedented fourth straight Eastern League title in 1999 with a huddle on the infield. Looking into the pack is Milton Bradley (28), whose two-out, two-strike grand slam in the bottom of the ninth inning accounts for the 12-11 victory over Norwich on a rainy, foggy and altogether surreal night on City Island.

Dave Trembley toils in the minors for 20 years before getting his chance in the majors

Chasing a Dream

"Your best shot may not be good enough on Monday, Tuesday or Wednesday, but Thursday is coming."

Pitcher **Willie Fordham** (1952)

Manager **Dave Trembley** (1987-89) before making his managerial debut in the majors for the Orioles on June 19, 2007 in San Diego:

"When I take the lineup card to home plate it will be a culmination of a lifelong dream. Maybe this will help motivate others to keep following their dreams."

"Double-A is a make-or-break year. If you can play here, you can play in the big leagues."

Catcher **Tom Prince** (1987)

itcher **Jim Tracy** (1989-90) after **Randy Tomlin** (1989-90) goes directly from Harrisburg to join the Pittsburgh Pirates in Philadelphia, where Tomlin throws a five-hitter to beat the Phillies 10-1 in his major league debut on Aug. 6, 1990:

"It keeps you sane. It shows you're not doing this for nothing. It gives you the reason why you're here, why you're going through all of this. The dream came true for him."

Tony Longmire (1988-90) in March 1992 on possibly replacing former two-time MVP **Dale Murphy** as the Philadelphia Phillies' right fielder:

"Nobody can ever step in for Dale Murphy. That's the type of guy he is. Maybe one day I'll go in and play for him, but I'll never be able to replace him."

"I'm driven to succeed where people think I can't. I wasn't supposed to get out of

TONY LONGMIRE

A-ball. I wasn't supposed to win the Triple-A batting title in 1979. When they first saw me as a player in Scottsdale, Arizona, in 1977 they weren't saying, 'This is a guy who's going to play in the big leagues in 1980.' That's what drives me to succeed."

Manager **Jim Tracy** (1993)

"I remember Davey Johnson telling me, 'You know, Trace, when you started here as my bench coach, I had no idea who the hell you were, or what you were capable of.' Now he tells me this three-quarters of the way into my second year with him in 2000. But then he says to me, 'I'm telling you now, there's no doubt in my mind that you're going to manage in the big leagues someday.' "

Jim Tracy (1993), who will manage in the majors from 2001-12

"I'd deliver water there just to get my foot in the door."

Pitcher **Steve Falteisek** (1995-96)

"I'm not leaving home for nine, 10 months a year to catch in the minor leagues for the rest of my life."
Catcher **Bob Henley** (1996-97)

"We tell these guys every day – and it starts to sound cliché – but as long as you have a uniform on, you have an opportunity. You never know what's going to happen."
Manager **Doug Sisson** (1999-2000)

Left-handed reliever **Ruben Niebla** (1998-99) on still bouncing around Class AA as he nears his 30th birthday in 2001:
"Hey, Jesse Orosco's clocking in another year and he's – what? – 42 years old, so that motivates me."

"You're not just playing for yourself and your organization, but there are scouts here from other teams and they see you, too."
First baseman-outfielder **Talmadge Nunnari** (1999-2001, 2003)

Pitcher **Troy Mattes** (1999-2000, 2003) on playing in 2005 for the independent league Lancaster Barnstormers:
"You see three kinds of guys on this level. You see guys looking for a first chance, guys looking for a second chance and guys just trying to hang on to the dream."

Shortstop **Brandon Phillips** (2001-02) on experiencing the majors for the first time with a spring training invitation in 2002:
"I can taste it, but I can't tell you what it takes like. But, honestly, it tastes pretty good. I'd probably say it tastes like chicken, because I love chicken."

Altoona manager **Dale Sveum** in 2001 on his former teammate in Pittsburgh and onetime Senator third baseman **John Wehner** (1990) becoming his new, 34-year-old utility player in Class AA:
"He's the kind of guy that's not going to give up baseball until his phone stops ringing."

Outfielder **Matt Cepicky** (2001-02) on the minor leagues being a stepping stone to reach the majors:

"I love playing in Harrisburg, but as a player you don't want to go back there."

"You realize that in Double-A you're not that far away. You can be playing with a guy for several months, then come into the clubhouse one day and he's not there because he's in the big leagues. You see that happen and you believe that it can happen to you. ... If I didn't think there was any chance of making the big leagues I wouldn't keep playing. Making the big leagues is why you play. And when I do make it there, it will be an unbelievable story."

Backup catcher **Jason Brown** (2002-04), who never made it there

"I like Harrisburg but the goal is to move up. I don't want any sandwiches named after me at Zembie's until I move up to the big leagues."

First baseman **Jeff Bailey** (2002-03)

"I don't want them to look at my birth certificate. I want them to look at my numbers. I want them to say, 'Damn, this kid is 30 but he can still run, throw and hit, so let's give him a chance.' "

Outfielder **Quincy Foster** (2002-03)

"You won't survive if you don't think you're going to make it. Everybody on this team knows they're going to be in the big leagues, even though the numbers say only a small percentage of us will make it. That's why I say, 'Fake it 'til you make it.' You've got to see yourself in the big leagues, otherwise you won't know what to do when you get there."

Pitcher **Aaron Thompson** (2010)

"There's a big misconception in baseball that we just show up for a 6:30 game at 6, strap it on and play. That's very far from the truth. We get up early, get out here early, and we work hard. Playing 142 games and having one or two days off a month, plus all the traveling, it's a lot tougher than people think it is."

Relief pitcher **Brett Campbell** (2006-07)

Living a Dream

"I came out of John Harris (High School) in 1929 and they called me to come to the island to pitch batting practice. I went over there and they watched me work, and after they watched me they signed me to a $200-a-month contract for the rest of the summer. Boy, was I a hot shot being a professional baseball player. What else was there?"

Pitcher **Lefty Hefflefinger** (1929, 1931-35)

Manager and heretofore minor league lifer **Dave Trembley** (1987-89) on Opening Day 2007 after reaching the majors as the Baltimore Orioles' bench coach; two months later, he replaces Sam Perlozzo as the slumping Orioles' interim manager:

"I'm 55 years old and I'm a rookie in the big leagues."

"One day in the big leagues makes it all worthwhile. I'd do it all again. ... I'll just be forever grateful for every day I get to be here."

Manager **Dave Trembley** (1987-89)

Montreal pitcher **Scott Ruskin** (1988-89) on being a major league rookie in 1990:

"There are still days when I just sit around somewhere and try to take in all of this. It's fantastic. It's more than you can imagine when you're in the minor leagues."

SCOTT RUSKIN

Manager **Pat Kelly** (1995-96) on being 17 years old in 1973 and catching for the short-season, Class A Idaho Falls Angels:

"I was traveling with 25 other guys on a bus and staying in hotels – and getting paid to play a game. I got to wear an old major league uniform and actually got paid on the first and the 15th of every month."

"I'll do this job until they pry the mike out of my dead hand."

Longtime City Island PA announcer Chris Andree

❝You have to take everything moment by moment. You shouldn't worry so much about what lies ahead at the end of the season or a year from now, because you really don't know where you're going to be."

Infielder **Jamey Carroll** (1998-2000, 2002)

"I play a game for a living. You're doing something a lot of people wish they could do. Your worst day is someone else's best day."

Catcher **Josh Emmerick** (2005-06)

Outfielder **Brandon Watson** (2002-03, 2005) on being a rookie with the Washington Nationals in 2005:

"You can't be picky when you're here, because here is where you want to be."

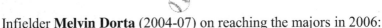

Infielder **Melvin Dorta** (2004-07) on reaching the majors in 2006:

"Up there you have everything you want. You still have to work hard, but there are a lot of people who are there to help you. Plus the guys you're facing are the guys you've been seeing on TV for a long time, like Tom Glavine, Greg Maddux … it's awesome."

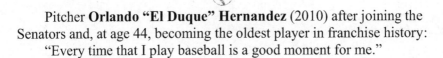

Pitcher **Orlando "El Duque" Hernandez** (2010) after joining the Senators and, at age 44, becoming the oldest player in franchise history:

"Every time that I play baseball is a good moment for me."

Ending a Dream

Montreal Expos manager and Hall of Famer Frank Robinson on the end of spring training and, for some, the end to dreams of million-dollar paydays:

"The last cuts are the hardest cuts of all. You know you have their futures in the palm of your hand. You know they may not be employed in baseball after that. That's what makes it so gut-wrenching."

"With the release, they give you some severance pay, a pat on the back and a piece of paper that says, 'See you later.' "
Catcher Bob Henley
Classes of 1996-97

"Once the game stops being fun, once you start going through the motions, then it's time to get another job."

Outfielder **Peter Bergeron** (1998-99)

First baseman **Jon Tucker** (1998-99) in December 1999 on contemplating ending his career:

"I'm still working out like I'm going to come back, but if I can find something else then why would I come back for another year in the minors? I like the game, but is it worth it? The long bus rides, being alone … is it worth it? I could get a normal job and not play baseball."

PETER BERGERON

Relief pitcher **Ruben Niebla** (1998-99) on being released in 1999:

"It's something you always expect. I'll get hooked up with another team, but it's a matter of if I want to play. I have a college degree. It might be time to put that to use."

Outfielder **Jeremy Ware** (1999-2004) on taking the roster spot of **Talmadge Nunnari** (1999-2001, 2003) when the popular first baseman-outfielder is released in April 2003:

"It happens to all of us at one time or another. You just hate to see this happen to a friend."

"I don't miss the sacrifices you have to make with your family and the sacrifices you have to make being away from home. I did that for so long, I got tired of making the sacrifices."

First baseman-outfielder **Talmadge Nunnari** (1999-2001, 2003)

Pitcher **Mark Mangum** (2001-02) on his midseason retirement in 2002 at age 23:

"I just tired of the battle. Whether I did well or not, it always was a battle. There was nothing at the end for me. I didn't get the reward. I believed I could have made it to the big leagues, but I didn't think it was worth the struggle. The only thing I could have gotten out of it was money, and that's not me. I wish I loved the game enough to stick with it."

Infielder **Dan DeMent** (2005-07) on the end of his playing career:

"I was kind of bitter for a while and still wanted to play. I know my age was getting up there, but I still had good numbers. It was a tough bullet to bite. … A lot of guys I played with are still playing, and it's not easy throwing them batting practice and hitting fungos at them when I should be hitting BP and taking fungos."

Reuben "Bud" Smitley in September 2012 on stepping down after 25 years as the Senators' Sunday Chapel leader:

"When memories become stronger than dreams it's time to move on, but I have great memories."

Cheating

Of steroids, spitters and corkers

Senators pitching coach **Tommy John** (2002), who during his 26-year career in the majors won 288 games with guile, sinkers and an occasional spitball, on steroids that were still permeating the game during his lone summer on City Island in 2002:

"I would have wanted (steroids) to take something away from me. I didn't want to go out there and throw hard. I wanted it to be less. I wanted to take something off of the pitch. People will say, 'Oh, well, he hit all of those home runs, therefore he's taking this.' Well, you still have to put the bat on the ball squarely. A guy can take steroids and he'll still hit my sinker into the ground; he'll just hit it harder and it will get to the shortstop faster."

"Amphetamines were the big thing back (in the 1960s and '70s). Everybody took 'greenies' but they didn't make you stronger. They just made you think you were stronger."

Pitching coach **Tommy John** (2002)

"I would be in favor after every ballgame to test each starting pitcher and take three guys in each lineup to test at random. I know when I played that I was clean. I just wanted to make sure the guy I was going against was clean, too. They do it in the Olympics and it keeps everything relatively equal."

Pitching coach **Tommy John** (2002)

Outfielder **Brandon Watson** (2002-03, 2005) on corking bats:
"People are going to use what they need to get where they want to get. I wouldn't put it past anybody."

"I guarantee you no one on this team is corking bats, but it's funny because we were just talking about getting a drill and see if we could do it. Just to see what it felt like."
Second baseman **Josh McKinley** (2002-04) after Chicago Cubs outfielder **Sammy Sosa** is caught using a corked bat in 2003

Struggling catcher **Scott Ackerman** (2000, 2002-03) on the benefits of a corked bat: "You have to actually hit the ball to make the cork work."

Cork: Best for bottles, not bats

Shortstop **Josh Labandeira** (2003-05) on being suspended for 15 games in 2005 for possessing amphetamines, despite never testing positive on a drug test:
"I reach the big leagues last season and my hometown paper writes nothing. I do this and I'm all over the front page. My mom said, 'I want to see your name in the paper, but not for this.' "

"It makes me afraid to go to places like GNC, and it forces you to stay away from things people have used in the past. As a player, you've got to know your stuff."
Outfielder **Mike Daniel** (2008-10)

"A 50-game suspension, I think, serves its purpose. You're going to be thoroughly embarrassed in the local publications, in *Baseball America*, in your organization and with your family. If that doesn't humble you and get your attention, then you're never going to be able to reach that person."
Nationals director of player development **Doug Harris**

SMILE ... YOU'RE ON CANDID CAMERA

As the Nationals celebrated their 2012 National League East title some well-meaning photographer snapped a shot of rookie outfielder Bryce Harper (2011, 2013) cracking open a bottle of champagne. Only one small problem: Harper – a self-proclaimed, non-drinker – was a most-definitely underage 19 at the time.

College Days

Pitcher **Justin Wayne** (2001-02) on the differences between playing collegiately at Stanford and professionally on City Island:
"It really hit home in my sophomore year. That's when I started realizing that, possibly, baseball could be more than just an after-school activity. It's a profession out here; it's your job."

Shortstop **Josh Labandeira** (2003-05) on his wife, former softball All-American Becky Witt, during their playing days at Fresno State:
"She has a way better career batting average than I did. She had an 0-for-28 slump in her senior year and still hit .400."

Crystal Balls

Public address announcer **Chris Andree** in the fall of 1998 on the prospects of the Senators winning a record-setting, fourth straight Eastern League title in 1999:
"Hey, we could call them the 'Quad Squad.' "

Doug Sisson holds back Milton Bradley after Bradley could not hold his tongue or gum

Infielder **Jamey Carroll** (1998-2000, 2002) after the Senators lose 13 of their first 18 games in a 1999 season that would end with their fourth straight EL championship:
"It's all right. We'll give everybody else a head start and then catch up at the end."

Manager **Doug Sisson** (1999-2000) the day after **Milton Bradley** (1999) is suspended for seven games after spitting gum at umpire Tim Pasch and five months before Bradley's beyond-dramatic grand slam gives the Senators a fourth straight title:
"I hope by the end of the year people are talking about what a special player Milton is and not just this."

Life as a DH helps Matt LeCroy earn $2.4 million in eight years in the major leagues

To DH or not to DH

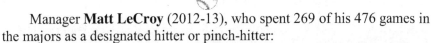

> **"I**f I had a choice, I'd rather catch. Being a DH is kind of boring. If you make a mistake, you think about it for nine hitters. If you're playing you go out and forget about it."
>
> Catcher **Bob Natal** (1991)

Manager **Matt LeCroy** (2012-13), who spent 269 of his 476 games in the majors as a designated hitter or pinch-hitter:

"I'm a big fan of the DH. I have five kids at home. If it wasn't for the DH they may not be eating right now."

Matt Stairs' prowess with the bat and his lack of a natural position with the glove for the Senators in 1991 made him an ideal DH and pinch hitter in the majors, where he spends 19 seasons from 1992-2011.

Dig the Long Ball

M anager **Dave Machemer** (2003-04) on making history on June 21, 1978, when during the California Angels' 5-2 victory at Minnesota he became the first player ever to bat leadoff in his major league debut and then homer to start the game:

"When I hit it, I knew it was gone. I was running to first and I'm watching the ball the whole way because I want to see if it's going to stay fair. As I'm looking for the ball and I'm looking for the umpire to make a signal, I run right by first base and never even touch it. ... I had to go back three steps and retouch the base."

Singles-hitting infielder **Jamey Carroll** (1998-2000, 2002) on his second major league homer, which caroms off the speakers hanging 120 above the field at Montreal's Olympic Stadium on Aug. 1, 2003:

"When I came around first base I saw the umpire give the home run signal. I don't hit them enough to be able to stand there – I've got to still run."

WHO KNEW?

The only home run hit by onetime Harrisburg Senators manager Luis Dorante (2001) during his playing career in Class AA came Aug. 23, 1991 on City Island as he helped New Britain to a 7-4 victory.

Outfielder **Dermal Brown** (2005) on hitting the last of his three homers in a game on June 11, 2005 – a solo homer to center field in the 10th inning that gives the Senators a 6-5 victory over Reading on City Island:

"The last one was a nice one because I could go home."

Manager **John Stearns** (2006, 2008-09) on the homer down the left-field line hit by **Ian Desmond** (2006, 2008-09) in a 6-5 victory at Reading on Opening Night 2009:

"That had to be 480 feet. When it went over the foul pole it was still 100 feet high in the air. That thing was a satellite in space."

ANDREW LINKER

Dollars and Sense

"There is a price for victory ... but well worth it, of course." Harrisburg mayor **Stephen Reed** after the city-owned Senators' expenses from their 1996 playoff run outpaced revenues by $12,795.

Harrisburg mayor **Stephen Reed** in December 1998 as the city-owned Senators make plans to spend $35,000 for 70 championship rings to give to players and staff:

"Ironically, it actually costs more money if you win the championship. ... From a purely economic side, the best thing is to get into the playoffs and then lose the last game."

Pitching coach **Bo McLaughlin** (1995-96) on whether he will spend the 1996 season with Class AAA Ottawa or be back in Class AA Harrisburg:

"My contract says, 'minor league pitching coach,' but the money says, 'Double-A,' so I guess I'll be back in Harrisburg."

BO McLAUGHLIN

Catcher **Bob Henley** (1996-97) on telling friends and family of his first-year, Class AA salary of $1,400 per month:

"Sometimes you want to avoid telling them, just to save face. Then when you tell them what you make, their eyes light up. They don't believe you."

"People sometimes are under the illusion that minor leaguers make a lot of money. Hey, we could make more at a real 9-to-5 job, but where else can you get paid to play a kids' game?"

Pitcher **Steve Falteisek** (1995-96)

"There are minor league franchises that actually lose money. You really have to foul things up to do that; you really have to alienate your community."

Senators business manager **Steven Resnick** (1996-99)

Harrisburg mayor **Stephen Reed** on the oft-controversial but financially productive reign of **Steven Resnick** as the Senators' business manager:

"I know he rubbed an awful lot of people the wrong way. Frankly, he wasn't here to win any popularity contests."

Relief pitcher and survivor of the paycheck-to-paycheck independent leagues, **Ruben Niebla** (1998-99) on facing Reading's Pat Burrell a year after Burrell receives a $3.15 million signing bonus from the Philadelphia Phillies:

"To me, he still was going to be an out. That's my mentality, but then once I did strike him out, it was kind of like, 'Oh, c'mon, you're making all that money.' "

Relief pitcher **Tim Dixon** (1997-99) volunteering to serve as an agent for **Javier Vazquez** after watching the Montreal Expos' top pitching prospect breeze through the Eastern League in 1997 with a 6-0 regular-season record on his way to a 14-year career in the majors:

"That's good money if I can get 5 percent of his contract."

IF ONLY ...

Had onetime Senators relief pitcher and Scott Boras wannabe Tim Dixon (1997-99) actually been Javier Vazquez's agent – and presuming Vazquez (1997) would have given him a 5-percent commission – the deal would have been worth $4.97 million to Dixon, based on Vazquez's $99.4 million in career earnings.

Before taxes, of course.

Esprit de Corps

"**P**eople from both sides of the river get together. The river is a big barrier in our community, but baseball is bringing us together."

Team president **Scott Carter** on the Susquehanna River

"I would have stayed in Harrisburg forever if the Pirates would have let me. Harrisburg was home for me. I'd go to coffee shops for breakfast and the people knew me. They made me feel important."

Manager **Dave Trembley** (1987-89)

"There are some places where people follow the team, but those people in Harrisburg are really fans. I watched that (1999) championship game on film. It's raining and I see all these people in the ballpark and I'm thinking, 'They're nuts.' But that's what makes it great. They get involved with the players."

Expos director of player development **Donnie Reynolds**

Mayor **Stephen Reed** on bringing back baseball to Harrisburg in 1987 after a 35-year absence:

"It brought together the East and West sides of the Susquehanna River in a way that hadn't been done in 30 years. You can do a lot for a city, but people don't get as excited about bricks and mortar … baseball is a rallying point for community spirit and pride."

Team president **Kevin Kulp** after the stadium completes its $45.1 million renovation in 2010:

"It will be an ongoing initiative to figure out ways to get more fans in this park, because as the saying goes, 'Empty seats don't buy any hot dogs.' "

Evaluating Talent

Manager **Dave Trembley** (1987-89) on his role in the minors:
"You shouldn't be measured by how many games you win or lose. Your worth should be determined on how you develop players for the higher levels."

Adam Wogan, Montreal's director of player development, in 2004 with the Senators en route to losing 90 of 142 games:
"There's not a (major league) team out there that truthfully says they would win 100 games at Double-A at the expense of developing players."

Manager **Keith Bodie** (2005) on separating prospects from wannabes:
"It's not the ability you have; it's the ability you use."

> *"Players in Double-A can see the light at the end of the tunnel. Players in Triple-A already have seen that light and have been run over by the train."*

Major league scout **Ben McLure** of Hummelstown

Manager **Keith Bodie** (2005) on players:
"All you can do is give people an opportunity, work hard with them and give them a chance to show what they can do. As a player that's all you want but, ultimately as a player, you have to go out there and perform."

ANDREW LINKER

Extreme Makeover

Senators broadcaster **Terry Byrom** in April 2010 on the $45.1 million renovations to Metro Bank Park, which used to be called Commerce Bank Park, which had been named RiverSide Stadium, which a century earlier was simply known as Island Park:

"When it's all said and done, we built a new ballpark. About 5 percent of the ballpark that existed before is there. Technically speaking, it's a renovation. But it'd be like you and I getting married and gutting the house except for the living room and, even then, expanding the living room from 400 square feet to 1,000 feet."

"It was very important that this ballpark not look like every other ballpark around. We're on an island. It's a unique setting. We wanted a unique ballpark."
Senators team president **Kevin Kulp**

"We used to have those troughs (in the men's room). Now we use them for planters around the ballpark."
Senators team president **Kevin Kulp**

Metro Bank Park in 2008 (above) and after its $45.1 million makeover in 2010

City Island's baseball field as it looks from the left-field line in the early 1900s

The ballpark, left, as seen from the outfield circa 1910 and then underwater after the 1936 flood that covers everything but the grandstand roof and light towers – seen next to the city's water filtration plant. The flood leaves the island without baseball until 1940.

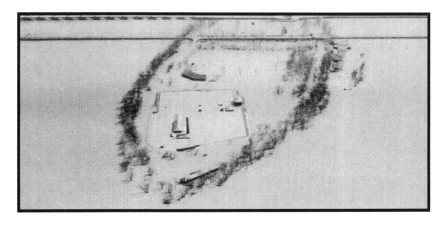

Island Park, above, during a pregame awards ceremony in the early 1950s; underwater again, thanks to the 1972 flooding from Hurricane Agnes; and during batting practice in 1987 with manager Dave Trembley pitching and an outfield backdrop looking remarkably similar to the one from the early '50s.

A top-of-the-grandstand look at the ballpark in the early 1900s, when the outfield – as it did for so many years after the Senators' return in 1987 – drains poorly from center to right; an artist's rendering (above, middle) of how RiverSide Stadium is supposed to look when it opens; and, left, how the stadium really looks less than three weeks before Opening Day in 1987. The grandstands and bleachers along the first-base and right field lines come later.

RiverSide Stadium, above, in all of its Spartan glory, during the Senators' return in 1987; pitching coach Spin Williams watches Rob Russell (6) work in the Senators' even-more Spartan bullpen in '87 – more than 20 years before boardwalks and beer decks – and RiverSide all grown up in 2013, by then known as Metro Bank Park.

Fame and Fortune

First baseman **Derrick White** (1992-93) in 1993 on roommate and future major league All-Star **Cliff Floyd** (1993):

"We'd get home and the phone would ring 20 times an hour. You would have agents calling, people you haven't heard from in four, five years calling. Everybody's tugging at you, wanting something. You have to recognize that. Cliff's done it so easily. It amazes me."

CLIFF FLOYD

First baseman-outfielder **Cliff Floyd** in 1993 on autograph seekers:

"It's strange to me that so many people know Cliff Floyd. It makes me feel good that they want my autograph. It's an honor when they want you to write your name on a baseball card or a piece of paper. How many kids would love to have that happen to them one day?"

Infielder **Jamey Carroll** (1998-2000, 2002) on hitting over .300 for the Rockies in 2006 and being a regular guest for a Denver radio show:

"You get a couple of hits and, all of a sudden, everybody wants to talk with you."

Pitcher **Stephen Strasburg** (2010-11) on receiving nearly all of the attention in 2010 while Harrisburg teammates and future major leaguers like **Tommy Milone** (2010), **Danny Espinosa** (2010) and **Drew Storen** (2009-10, 2012) are mostly overlooked by the media:

"I wish (the media) had a little more excitement for some of the other players on this team. The big attraction is all the hype and being the No. 1 pick and being in the limelight, but we have some really talented guys in this organization and that really needs to be shown to the world."

Family Portraits

"**M**y family is everything to me. The game is just a small part of me that I really love, but my true calling is being a father. ... If I retire it's not because I can't play anymore; it's because I can't stand being away from them anymore. And every year it gets much, much tougher. I tell my daughter, 'Every day I'm away from you I get two more gray hairs.' "

Pitcher **Joey Eischen** (1993) in 2006, his final season

General manager **Todd Vander Woude** on the birth of his daughter, Kristen, in August 1993:

"She was 2 ½ weeks early. She was due on Lunch Bag Night."

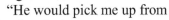

Pitcher **Tony Armas Jr.** (1999) on traveling to Boston to play in the inaugural Futures Game in 1999 at Fenway Park, where his father was a power-hitting outfielder in the 1980s:

"He would pick me up from school and take us to the ballpark. I was growing up next to big league guys. I hope things haven't changed too much."

JUNIOR

SENIOR

Catcher **Bob Henley** (1996-97) in 2004 on beating his then-toddler daughter Anna in a game of Candyland:

"I'll never let her just win. She'll enjoy it more when she wins on her own."

Former Senators left-hander **Jake Chapman** (2000-01) in 2008 on the thought of pitching to his sons Camden, then 6, and Colby, 4:

"If my kids are lefty, watch out. I'm going to throw sliders to them on every pitch."

F ormer National League All-Star second baseman **Tom Herr** on taking himself out of consideration to become the Senators' manager in 2000:

"I've been around baseball long enough and seen enough families destroyed by guys during their playing days, and by coaches and managers who have put the game ahead of their families. That has made me think twice about this, about putting that strain on my family."

Manager **Dave Machemer** (2003-04) on receiving $1,000 in airline vouchers from the Senators after his 1,000th career victory in 2003:

"I'm going to take my wife to Hawaii for our 28th anniversary. I would have taken her there for our 25th, but I didn't have $1,000."

Pitcher **Chris Young** (2003) on his wedding to Liz Patrick:

"She's upset because starting next year, she knows it's going to be St. Young's Day instead of St. Patrick's Day."

Catcher **Bob Henley** (1996-97) in 2004 on the prospects of his wife Katina, a captain in the Army Reserve, being deployed to Iraq:

"I would feel a little selfish wanting her to stay here, because you see all these young men and women dying, and they're just as special to their families as my wife is to me."

Infielder **Dan DeMent** (2005-07) on how he used the $1,000 signing bonus he received in 2000 from Tampa Bay:

"I spent it right away for my wife's engagement ring. It was a good investment. It's worked out well so far."

Manager **Matt LeCroy** (2012-13) on his players:

"I call them my boys. I have five kids at home, but I have 25 kids up here. I think of them that way, like they're my own kids."

Manager **Dave Machemer** (2003-04) on his son's plans to run with the bulls in Pamplona:

"If you're watching it on television and you see a red-headed kid with a horn up his ass, that's my son, David."

Fashion Statements

6 6 **I** feel a whole lot more comfortable in a baseball uniform than I do in a suit and tie."

Manager **Dave Trembley** (1987-89)

F.P. Santangelo (1991), then a utility player with Montreal, on the teasing he withstood in 1998 when his Expos teammates learned that his old jersey No. 24 was being retired at Class AAA Ottawa:

"They're just jealous they didn't play in Triple-A for 22 years."

F.P. SANTANGELO

Manager **Rick Sofield** (1997) on shivering through another cold April in the Eastern League:

"If there's a fire in my hotel, I wouldn't lose anything. Half of the time, I'm wearing everything I own."

Pitching coach **Brent Strom** (1998) on winning 22 games during his five-year career in the majors:

"That was my uniform number most of the time, too. If I had known I was going to do that, I would have asked for Number 315."

Catcher-third baseman **Michael Barrett** (1998) on talking with St. Louis first baseman Mark McGwire after picking up a single during his rookie call-up with the Expos in September 1998:

"He acknowledged my existence and that was exciting. Then McGwire saw I had on my lucky shirt from Harrisburg beneath my Montreal jersey and he says to me, 'Hey, you're here now; you have to get rid of that thing.' Then in the process of all this, I missed a steal sign."

When infielder Jason Camilli was summoned from Harrisburg to Class AAA Ottawa in early July 1999 he left behind his jersey No. 18.

The number was quickly claimed by Rick Sweet, the Senators' interim manager who wore No. 18 just a year earlier when Harrisburg won its third straight Eastern League title.

Sweet, though, was not the only one interested in Camilli's jersey. First baseman-outfielder Talmadge Nunnari also put in a claim for it.

Sweet was sympathetic, sort of, to Nunnari's request and offered one of his best hitters another option for wearing No. 18.

TALMADGE NUNNARI

"I told him," Sweet said, "that he could go back to (Class A) Jupiter if he really wanted it."

More time with the Senators in 2002 has Jamey Carroll looking for a luckier number

Outfielder **Kenny James** (1999-2001), known for his sartorial splendor, on being told he may have been outdone when manager **Luis Dorante** wore a three-piece, cream-colored suit to the team's 2001 preseason banquet:

"Yeah, he looks clean now, but how many of those can he pull out of the closet?"

Infielder **Jamey Carroll** (1998-2000, 2002) on wearing No. 19 for his brief, three-game stay with the Senators in 2002:

"That's my mother's birthday, so I had to take that number. Now I have to see if she has any hits left in her."

A glimpse into the trailer that doubles as the Senators' clubhouse in 1987

Scoreboard operator **Nate Austin** on the Senators' tie-dyed jerseys with their uniform numbers centered in a multi-colored bull's-eye for a Parrothead Night promotion on June 4, 2003:
"They shouldn't wear those by an archery range."

Pitcher **Danny Rueckel** (2004-07) on wearing a Montreal Expos home white jersey with his Senators' red-and-black trimmed pants at the 2004 Eastern League All-Star Game in Bowie:
"We have every color you can think of on our bodies right now, and none of it matches."

DANNY RUECKEL

Josh Labandeira (2003-05), the 5-foot-7 shortstop, on receiving jersey No. 1 when he joined the Montreal Expos for the final two weeks of the 2004 season:
"You have to give the smallest guy the smallest number."

Hitting coach **Rob Ducey** (2004) on switching to No. 6 after his familiar No. 2 jersey shows up missing:
"I've worn 40 before and went to 20, and became half the man I used to be. Now I'm going from 2 to 6, so I'm going to be three times the man I used to be."

Floodwaters

L et's see. You play baseball on an island in a middle of a river that stretches from Cooperstown, N.Y., to the Chesapeake Bay and has been known to flood more times than not. What could go wrong?

Most times, the flooding along the Susquehanna River comes from the winter thaw of upstate New York, a mess that comes before the season and leaves the Senators' grounds crew – if those folks are lucky – a few days to clean up before the start of another season.

Sometimes, the flooding is really bad, as it was in March 1936 when the surging Susquehanna spilled into the ballpark and put the Senators out of business for four years. Then there was the late-season flooding in 2011 that forced the Eastern League-leading Senators to play their postseason home games on the road in Richmond, Va.

"It wasn't so much the damage (in 2011), it was just stuff. So much crap came in. There was trash everywhere. Every empty water bottle from New York and northern Pennsylvania found its way here."

General manager **Randy Whitaker**

"There was a sense of calm because of the grounds crew," team president ***Kevin Kulp*** *said of the 2011 flood. "It's like they brought their lunch pails and boots and never complained. I would have been a wreck."*

GM **Randy Whitaker** on the stadium's post-flood aroma in 2011:
"The best way I can describe it is it smelled like a dog kennel. I went home with it in my nose."

Some of Tim Foreman's fine-feathered friends getting ready to help pull tarp on a flooded field just days before the 1997 season opener

The Sod God

B ones Boss ruled the place 100 years earlier, taking care of Island
Park as if it were his own. So much so that the ashes of his body
eventually were scattered on the field he once manicured.

Turns out that Boss had a worthy successor, a onetime college catcher
named Tim Foreman who arrived on City Island in 1994 and made the
place his home. You'll know him when you see him; he's the one covered
in dirt, grime and God knows what else he encounters on a daily basis.

Kent Qualls, the Montreal Expos' director of minor league operations
in the mid-1990s, used to look for Foreman by searching for the filthiest-
looking person in the ballpark.

"We didn't know sometimes if he had a tan or if he was just covered
in dirt," Qualls said.

Stadium operations director **Tim
Foreman** on first seeing the ballpark under
layers of snow, water, mud and trash following the historic January '96 blizzard
and flood:

"When I first came in and saw it, I
said, 'Oh, God.' I had my doubts."

TIM FOREMAN

Groundskeeper **Brandon Forsburg**
on Foreman's leadership in preparing to
unearth the stadium after the flood of
2011:

"He sat everybody down and told us to get the shock and awe factor
out of the way. He was very calm."

"For me, only working an eight-hour day is like a vacation."
Stadium Operations Director **Tim Foreman**

Foreign Legion

Manager **Dave Jauss** (1994) in December 1996 on spending a rare offseason with his family in the United States rather than coaching in the Venezuelan Winter League:
"It's been great the last three months. We have a new son, a new house and we're in the States for the first time this winter. I had to explain to my kids how Halloween worked."

Pitcher **Kirk Bullinger** (1995-97) on playing winter ball:
"I heard playing in Puerto Rico wasn't so bad. I heard they have good water and good food, and I heard they have good cable. I got to have my ESPN."

KIRK BULLINGER

Manager **Doug Sisson** (1999-2000) on the troubles of infielder **Albenis Machado** (2001-03) getting around in his native, but strife-torn, Venezuela in the winter of 2002:
"We worry about things every day like where we're going to dinner that night and how nice the restaurant is going to be. They're worried about if they're going to wake up the next day alive or if they can go out in public without somebody accosting them or if they can get gas for their car."

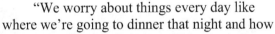

Manager **Dave Machemer** (2003-04) on the travails of traveling the roads of Venezuela during his time there as a winter ball manager:
"People there have no regard for driving. They're either cutting out in front of you or they're coming at you."

Gloving Words

D uring his 10 seasons in the major leagues from 1946-55, **Billy Cox**, the third baseman from Newport, Pa., whose pro career started on City Island in 1940, had no peer in the field.

That was never more evident than in the 1952 World Series, when Cox and the Brooklyn Dodgers lost in seven games to the New York Yankees.

Cox flawlessly fielded 23 of 24 chances in that Series with his only error leading to no runs for New York.

"That ain't a third baseman," Yankees manager Casey Stengel said. "That's a f-----g acrobat.

BILLY COX

"I take it personally when they steal. Nothing feels better than watching a guy run off the field after you've thrown him out."

Catcher **Brian Schneider** (1999)

Infielder **Jason Camilli** (1998-2000) after committing a single-game, franchise-record five errors while playing third base in a 6-4 victory over Binghamton on May 14, 2000 at RiverSide Stadium:

BRIAN SCHNEIDER

"You can't say, 'I don't want the ball hit at me.' You have to want that ball. You want that pitcher to get confidence back in you."

Manager **Matt LeCroy** (2012-13), a backup catcher for the Nationals in 2006, on being pulled from a game against Houston after allowing six stolen bases and making two throwing errors:

"If my daddy was managing this team, I'm sure he would have done the same thing."

God Bless 'Em

How prayer plays in the game

"I f you're a quiet person, people may think you're not a competitive person. If you're quiet and you're a Christian, then you're an easy mark."

Pitcher **Bill Sampen** (1988-89)

"Jesus would have been a very aggressive pitcher."

Pitcher **Lee Hancock** (1990)

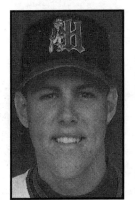

"To have a strong spiritual side only strengthens you as an athlete. There are ups and downs in the game, and to know there's a higher being guiding your life keeps you grounded."

Pitcher **Neil Weber** (1995-97)

NEIL WEBER

"When I was in Class A ball the coaches thought I was scared to come inside on guys because I didn't want to hurt them. That was funny to me, because that year and every year since I've led the team in hit batsmen. ... I pitch inside, because that's the way the game is played. Throwing inside is not anywhere outside of what I believe in as a Christian. There's nowhere in the Bible that says you don't do a job the way it's supposed to be done."

Pitcher **Mark Mangum** (2001-02)

"(Baseball Chapel) is the greatest thing that's ever happened in baseball, simply because if you want to go to church this gives you a chance to reflect, to pray and to hear somebody talk. You're here for a reason. Somebody – whomever you pray to – gave you tremendous ability. You should take that time to thank him ... or her."

Pitching coach **Tommy John** (2002)

"One baseball executive in the '80s said he had to get rid of some players on his team because they had too many Christians in the clubhouse and they weren't tough enough. That's the most idiotic, ignorant, ill-informed statement I ever heard from someone who went to college – and I knew the guy."

Pitching coach **Tommy John** (2002)

"There's a misconception people have that Christian athletes are weak and feeble. We want to show God's mercy, but we will not step down from a challenge."

Pitcher **Erik Arnesen** (2009-11)

Going to the Show

Pitcher **Randy Tomlin** (1989-90) on how he was told of his promotion to the major leagues on Aug. 6, 1990:

"I was polishing my shoes when (manager **Marc Bombard**) said, 'You want to put those down and have a seat.' Then he asked me if I ever heard of Veterans Stadium. I said yes. He said, 'Good, because you're pitching there Monday night.' "

RANDY TOMLIN

"You don't know how you're going to react when you finally get that call, but I can tell you I had tears of joy."

Pitcher **Joe Ausanio** (1990, 1993)

Manager **Tony Beasley** (2011) in 2012 on telling wunderkind out-fielder **Bryce Harper** (2011, 2013) – both then at Class AAA Syracuse – he was heading to the majors:

"It was a great honor to give him that call. You could tell he was excited and humbled by it. He was at a loss for words."

STEPHEN STRASBURG

Golden Arm

T he arm belongs to **Stephen Strasburg** (2010-11). Surely, you have heard of him. If not, how did you ever get this far in the book?

No prospect preceding him to City Island arrived with as much hype and as many expectations as Strasburg, the right-handed pitcher who had been an Olympian in 2008 and the first overall pick in the 2009 amateur draft.

Stephen Strasburg (2010-11) on the attention he received after signing with the Nationals for a record $13.1 million out of college:

"That contract stuff is not that important for me; it really isn't. I play this game because I love it. I don't play for the contract."

"I've seen people ask him to pet their dogs, to sign anything and everything. He has to feel like he's in a circus."

Outfielder **Mike Daniel** (2008-10) in April 2010

Stephen Strasburg (2010-11) on advice he would give to kids who want to be the next Stephen Strasburg:

"I would tell them to enjoy the experience. Unfortunately, not everybody is going to be able to play professional baseball, but it's not that big of a deal to me. What is big are the memories I have, the teammates I played with and the experiences I shared with them. That's something I really stress with the kids. Just go out and have fun. Enjoy it now, because it's not going to be there forever for them. And it's not going to be there forever for me either, so I'm just trying to enjoy it now."

"He's the only guy I've ever played with that lives up to the stories you hear. You hear stories about guys, and then you see them and go, 'Oh, I don't know.' But he lives up to everything they've said."

Closer **Drew Storen** (2009-10, 2012)

Stephen Strasburg (2010-11) on ignoring the paparazzi-like attention he received before, during and after his time on City Island:

"Everybody has their own opinion on me, and they can keep those opinions. I have my own."

"Around the locker room, he's just another guy. I mean, he's the guy we always want on the mound, but he's just another guy. We just see him as 'Strasburg.' We don't really care about the hype; we just treat him normally, and that's what he wants."

Closer **Drew Storen** (2009-10, 2012)

Stephen Strasburg (2010-11) on rehabbing his arm after undergoing Tommy John ligament transplant surgery in August 2010:

"I want to be the best at everything and right now I want to be the best at rehabbing and getting back out there. ... I've got great support all around me, and they reminded me of everything I should be thankful for, and they put everything in perspective for me. Bottom line, this is a game. I'm very blessed to play this game for a living. It's a minor setback, but in the grand scheme of things it's just a blip on the radar screen."

Manager Jim Tracy and the '93 Senators pose with the trophy for the EL's best regular-season record; they soon add bigger and better hardware in the playoffs.

Greatest Ever

Montreal general manager Dan Duquette had a prevailing thought when he was stocking the lower ends of the Expos' minor league system in 1990 and '91.

Geez, that Harrisburg team is going to be awfully good come 1993.

Turns out he was right, big time.

The '93 Senators were stunningly talented and equally successful.

They were a team loaded with premium draft picks and a manager in Jim Tracy who had something to prove after being unceremoniously fired by Cincinnati's impetuous general manager, Jim Bowden, despite Tracy's success in running the Reds' farm system.

All Tracy's '93 Senators did were win 100 games – 94 in the regular season and six more in the playoffs – with a team that Minor League Baseball would later honor as one of its top 100 teams in the 20th century.

"We have an attitude that we're good," first baseman-outfielder Cliff Floyd said early that season, "but we're also going to go out there and prove we're good."

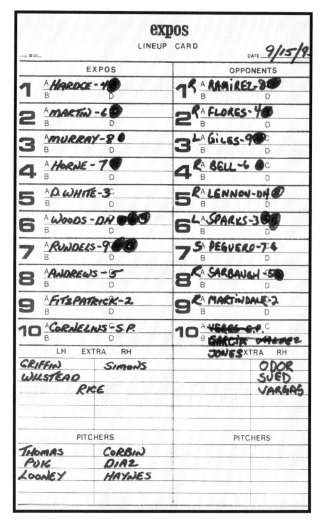

Manager Jim Tracy's dugout lineup card from the deciding
Game 5 of the 1993 Eastern League finals in Canton, Ohio

"It's so easy pitching for this team. This team scores early and they score late, and they score in bunches."

Pitcher **Reid Cornelius** (1991-93)

Manager **Jim Tracy** (1993) on the Senators reaching the season's midway point with a 52-18 record before winning 42 of their final 68 regular-season games:

"It's a pretty obnoxious record, isn't it?"

Happy Birthday

Manager **Dave Jauss** (1994) scoffing at the age of journeyman infielder **Edgar Tovar** (1993, 1995) who was listed as 19 years old on the Senators' 1993 Opening Day roster:
"Edgar? Edgar hasn't been 19 in 10 years."

Infielder **David Post** (1997-99) on growing up in Kingston, N.Y., not far from onetime Senators pitcher **Joe Ausanio** (1990, 1993):
"I remember him. He used to umpire my Little League games."

Pitching coach **Jerry Reuss** (2000) on the longevity of his career in the majors that lasted from 1969-90:
"A lot of guys I'm going to coach haven't been on the Earth as long as I played."

History Lessons

Pitching coach **Tommy John** (2002) on meeting players whose careers were saved by "Tommy John surgery," the revolutionary ligament transplant procedure named for him in the mid-1970s:
"A lot of people think Tommy John was the surgeon. A lot of ballplayers in this day and age really don't follow the history of baseball. They play it and they like it, but they couldn't tell you who played on the '86 Mets."

Andy Tracy (1998-99) makes his own history on City Island in 1999, when he hits an all-time franchise record 37 home runs while coming within one RBI of matching Joe Munson's Harrisburg record of 129 set during his Triple Crown season in 1925.

Help Wanted

Or how I spent my winter vacation

Manager **Jim Tracy** (1993) on one of his many part-time jobs after his playing career ended in the early 1980s:

"When you have a Dodge Omni and Sunday comes around – and you load that thing up with 400 Sunday (Chicago) Tribunes and you have front-wheel drive – well, you just kind of hope and make sure your front wheels have contact with the ground."

Pitcher **Tommy Phelps** (1996-99) on waiting tables at Big City Tavern in West Palm Beach after being released during the 1999 season:

"You can make pretty good money there, about 200 bucks a night for five hours work, but I want to compete. I don't want to bus tables all my life."

TOMMY PHELPS

Pitcher **Bryan Hebson** (2000-02) after working at a local eatery back home in Auburn, Ala.:

"You go into a locker room and you say whatever you want. But then a guy in the restaurant comes up to me and tells me where to go, and I just have to bite my lip."

BRYAN HEBSON

Pitcher **Chuck Crumpton** (2000-04) on spending his offseasons as a substitute teacher at his hometown high school in Mesquite, Tex.:

"There were quite a few teachers who I didn't get along with in high school and they're still there. When I went back there, they were all very nice. They were like, 'Well, he's grown up now. He's a normal human being, not a smart-ass jock running around school.'"

Hitting

After going hitless in all of his 34 at-bats for Harrisburg in 2001, outfielder **Troy Gingrich** (2001-03) finally picked up a single to center in his first Class AA at-bat in 2002 before heading back to Class A Brevard County. Naturally, Gingrich – a lifetime .231 hitter in four minor league seasons – eventually served as the Senators' hitting coach – and a well-respected one, too – from 2008-11.

"My motto is to go up to the plate and swing as hard as I can. Not wild and crazy swings, but nice and hard and aggressive."
First baseman-outfielder Cliff Floyd (1993)

CLIFF FLOYD

Manager **Dave Jauss** (1994) in June 1994 on his three top hitters – shortstop **Mark Grudzielanek** (1994), right fielder **Kevin Northrup** (1994-95) and first baseman **Randy Wilstead** (1993-94) – batting a combined .350 after two months of the season:

"Right now they're swinging the bat well, but all it takes is good pitching to Stop them. I'll tell you what, if those three guys hit .380 this year, I'll kiss your ass."

"They can put the strike zone wherever – on third base, in left field. It doesn't matter to me."

Right fielder **Vladimir Guerrero** (1996)

Light-hitting outfielder **Ed Bady** (1997-98) on his advice to pitcher **Scott Mitchell** (1997-99, 2001) before Mitchell's first career at-bat in 1997:

"I told him to focus on the emblem on the pitcher's cap, because the ball will likely be coming from near there. Then I thought, 'Hey, why haven't I been doing that?' "

ED BADY

"The key to a good season is getting hits when you're not swinging the bat well and getting them in bunches when you are."

Outfielder **Brad Wilkerson** (1999-2000)

"I don't mind hitting with two strikes. I know I get a lot of my hits with two strikes, and I know I'm going to get a lot of fastballs. Partly because I weigh 165, partly because I'm hitting .215."

Shortstop **Josh Reding** (2000-02)

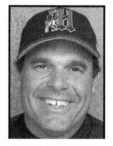

Hitting coach **Frank Cacciatore** (2002, 2005) on performing in the clutch:

"There's nothing more beautiful than a two-out base hit."

Cacciatore on his not-so-beautiful pupils:

"Some of my best work is out there pumping gas right now."

FRANK CACCIATORE

WHEN SECOND IS BEST

Prior to the Yankees' Robinson Cano joining them in 2013, only five second basemen had ever hit .300 or better in at least five straight full seasons in the majors. The first four – Eddie Collins, Charlie Gehringer, Rogers Hornsby and Rod Carew – are in the Hall of Fame. The fifth: Former Senator Jose Vidro (1995-1996) with the Expos from 1999-2003.

Home Sweet Home

Hard to believe, but not everyone loved RiverSide Stadium, the centerpiece of Harrisburg mayor Stephen Reed's grand plan in the mid-1980s to turn the slum that City Island had become into 63 acres of family-oriented fun.

Critics of the quaint little ballpark in the middle of the Susquehanna River tended to be opposing ballplayers who loathed camping out in the undersized clubhouses and managers who watched routine fly balls carry over the left-field wall, thanks to the prevailing winds blowing down river.

Construction foreman Bill Starsinic Sr. gave an insight into things to come before the stadium opened in April 1987.

"I've been here most of the winter, and down river is the wind direction," he said in March 1987. "This place is like a wind tunnel."

"This is a horrible park. The balls actually take hops at right angles. I've never seen anything like it. This is Class AA baseball and you can't play that caliber of baseball on this field. I'd expect something like this in the rookie league. I feel sorry for the Harrisburg team. You can't play baseball here; you just try to survive."

Glens Falls manager **Tom Burgess** in 1987

Pittsburgh player development director **Buzzy Keller** in April 1988 after the Senators add seats behind home plate, cutting the distance to the backstop from the recommended 60 feet to only 53 feet:

"I hate to see a good, regulation ballpark made into something else. Somebody sacrificed the rule book for a few more seats."

John Boles, Expos' player-development director, in January 1991:

"It's such an honest park. There are no quirks like a short right-field porch or thin air like Denver that can muddle a player's statistics. What a guy hits here is what he's going to hit. That's one of the reasons we like it here."

Manager and Illinois native **Mike Quade** (1991-92) after the Senators lift four homers into the down-river wind during a 9-6 victory over Hagerstown on Aug. 4, 1991:

"There are days when RiverSide Stadium turns into Wrigley Field."

Manager **Rick Sofield** (1997) on City Island's oft-blustery conditions:

"Every time contact is made and the ball heads to left field, we're not sure if it's going to be a home run or a pop-up to the shortstop."

MIKE QUADE

New Britain manager **Stan Cliburn** after his outfielders lose fly ball after fly ball during a 2002 series on City Island:

"I don't know what it is here. Maybe, it's the backdrop. The seats are tin-colored."

After his first 200 at-bats with the Senators in 2001, shortstop and future major league All-Star **Brandon Phillips** (2001-02) finds himself hitting only .210 on City Island with two homers and nine RBIs, compared to batting .365 on the road with three homers and 20 RBIs:

"It's not like I hate the place. It's just something about playing at home. I don't know; maybe I just like to travel."

Randy Tomlin on playing at old RiverSide Stadium with the Senators in 1989 and '90 before returning in 2010 as their pitching coach after the stadium undergoes a $45.1 million facelift:

"A lot of it was still the same from the last time I was here. Now this is a new time to create new memories."

Idol Moments

Pitcher **Jimmie DeShong** (1929-30) on joining the New York Yankees in 1934 and seeing Babe Ruth for the first time:

"I was standing next to Earle Combs, the outfielder, and I saw a napkin on a chair in front of Babe's locker. I asked Combs what it was. Hor d'oeuvres or something like that, he said. I went over and looked. There were six hot dogs. Six turned out to be nothing. I was told Babe once ate 24 between games of a doubleheader."

JIMMIE DeSHONG

Manager **Jim Tracy** (1993) on becoming Felipe Alou's bench coach in Montreal before the 2005 season:

"I was awed by the way Felipe Alou carried himself. I was totally impressed with him. I had watched him play baseball. I had his baseball card when I was 6 years old."

Shortstop **Mark Grudzielanek** (1994) on starting the 1994 Class AA All-Star Game in Binghamton, N.Y.:

"When I first came into the locker room, I said, 'Awesome' ... just to be playing with these guys. Then once I got on the field I said, 'Hey, I belong here.' "

Bob Henley (1996-97) on catching Lee Smith in the Expos' bullpen before the then-career saves leader works in a spring training game in 1997:

"For some guys, it's not a very big deal, but he's going to the Hall of Fame. You look up to those guys. After he threw that bullpen, I kept the ball. Stuck it in my back pocket. I got him to sign it. I'll keep that one, just as a reminder in case I never get to play with him."

Reliever **Rodney Stevenson** (1998-2000) on teammate **Donnie Bridges** (2000-02, 2004-05), the Eastern League's best starting pitcher in 2000:

"He is 'The Man.' The rest of us are stepsons."

Pitching coach and longtime major leaguer **Jerry Reuss** (2000), who gave up the most homers of any left-hander to Hall of Famer Mike Schmidt, on living during the 2000 season in the West Shore home of a Philadelphia Phillies fan:

"My room is like a shrine to the Phillies. I get up every day and stare at a poster of Mike Schmidt. If Schmidt knew, he'd laugh his ass off."

Independent Living

Pitcher **Joey Eischen** (1993) on playing for $1,500 per month in 1999 at Glens Falls of the independent Northern League:

"It's the same game there. I play because I love competing. I think I can say I had more fun in Glens Falls than anyplace else. There, it was pure baseball, no politicking."

"I had more fun playing in the Northern League than I've had probably since I played in Harrisburg. That really refreshed my love for the game. I stopped worrying and just started playing again."

JOEY EISCHEN

Pitcher **Joey Eischen** (1993)

"I'm the poster boy for the Western Baseball League. I was signed twice out of there (by Montreal and Los Angeles). When I went back there, I went back as a celebrity."

Relief pitcher **Ruben Niebla** (1998-99)

Keeping Score

"I was still wet behind the ears, and I wasn't the most popular guy in the clubhouse."
Charlie Robertson on being 18 years old and serving as the Senators' official scorekeeper in 1952 – 42 years before becoming the mayor of nearby York.

Sometimes cheerful, sometimes not, pitching coach **Bo McLaughlin** (1995-96) on first meeting backup official scorer **John Bricker**:
"Oh, you must be the other blind son of a bitch."

Kismet

Hard-luck relief pitcher **Jeff McAvoy** (2002) on fracturing a bone in his right foot after starting to turn around his season during a 48-hour span in which he wins a game in relief for the Senators, ends that same game by hitting a walk-off home run and then saves another game:
"This pretty much stays in line with the way things have gone this season for me. Just something else to put in the Jeff McAvoy file."

"We were like the 'Bad News Bears' out there. Anything that could happen did happen, and none of it was good for us."
Manager **Dave Machemer** (2003-04)

Infielder **Scott Hodges** (2000-02, 2005) on battling Hodgkin's Disease in 2005:
"It's a mind-over-matter thing. When you put your mind to it and say, 'I'm going to beat this' and go full throttle, then you can do anything."

Language Barrier

❝ I t's difficult to hang around someone when you don't understand what he's saying."

Shortstop **Rico Rossy** (1989)

Manager **Pat Kelly** (1995-96) on a 1996 team comprised of players from across the globe, including future major leaguers **Vladimir Guerrero**, **Jose Vidro**, **Izzy Alcantara**, **Jolbert Cabrera** and **Alex Pacheco**:

"It's a very eye-opening experience to realize what a Latin player goes through in this country. It's difficult just doing the simple things like ordering food and getting your mail. Things we take for granted become very difficult for them because of the language."

"For me, language is not a problem. When you're talking baseball, you understand pretty fast."

Dominican-born **Vladimir Guerrero** (1996)

CHRIS STOWERS

Geoff Blum in 1996, when his locker on City Island is sandwiched between those of Spanish-speaking teammates **Jose Vidro**, **Jolbert Cabrera**, **Vladimir Guerrero** and **Ramsey Koeyers**:

"For the most part, I'm going solo there. All the situations on the field are universal. Off the field, it's more trouble for them; they have to learn to adapt to us."

Outfielder **Chris Stowers** (1997-98) on helping his Spanish-speaking teammates off the field:

"I would always order food for them here. If they wanted pizza, I would order it for them. I didn't think anything of it. But playing winter ball down there in the Dominican Republic, when I had to order pizza, I realized how hard it really is for them to do it here."

> ## *"We may laugh at their English, but they laugh at our Spanish."*
> Infielder **Geoff Blum** (1996, 1998)

Senators manager and Brooklyn native **Keith Bodie** (2005) on his distinct dialect:

"People ask me about my accent all the time. I tell them that in Boston, 'You paaak your car. In Brooklyn, we steal your car.' "

Vladimir Guerrero never ventures far on City Island in 1996 without a translator. In this case, trainer Alex Ochoa helps out with a local television interview.

Geoff Blum (1996, 1998) on his difficulties speaking with Japanese teammates while playing fall ball in Hawaii:

"After a while, I just reverted to sign language."

Leadership

"**G**uys lead in different ways. More times than not for me, a guy that becomes a leader on the club does it by his attitude and by his performance. If you're a real gung-ho guy and only hitting .180, it's tough to lead. If you're putting up the numbers and you're playing hard every day, then leadership comes naturally."

Senators manager **Mike Quade** (1991-92)

"I asked my players to check their egos at the door. I did, too. If I'm asking people who are going to perform from day to day to check their egos, then why in the world wouldn't I?"

Manager **Jim Tracy** (1993)

"Everybody has their own type of personality, but **Jim Tracy** (1993) has a way to deal with all of them. He has an easy-going personality that could really crack a tough egg. He has a way with words."

Manager **Dave Machemer** (2003-04)

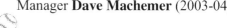

"I love reading about some of the more successful people in the industry I'm in. The Whitey Herzogs. The Jim Leylands. The Sparky Andersons. The thing to me that's consistent about every one of those guys is that they know it's the players who make them good. You put them in a position to win, and then let them go out and win. I did that in 1993 in Harrisburg. I didn't throw any pitches or get any hits or lay down any bunts. I'm just there to point a group of guys in the right direction."

Manager **Jim Tracy** (1993)

"There's no room for fear in the game. It's like raising your children. You don't want them to fear you; you want them to trust and respect you. Trust and respect are the two most important things in any relationship, whether you're married or you're a father or a priest or a baseball manager. If you don't have trust and respect, why would anybody listen to you?"

Manager **Keith Bodie** (2005)

Learning Curve

First baseman-outfielder **Cliff Floyd** (1993) on growing up during the 1980s in rugged south Chicago:
"You have a lot of gangs, a lot of violence, a lot of people who were jealous. Trying to stay off the streets was tough because you want to have fun. You're still young. You don't want to stop having fun just because guys are shooting guns. … But you hear gunshots at nighttime and you tell yourself,' One day, I have to get out of here.' "

Olivia Floyd on raising her son in south Chicago:
"It was not so much the gangs but the drug dealers. In our neighborhood, the kids worried about those shirts and shoes. Guys were always offering, 'If you do this for us, then we'll do this for you.' He had to avoid that peer pressure. I would tell Clifford, 'I know some of your friends are doing illegal things; I don't want you to do the same.' But they would tell him, 'Cliff, we're doing these things, but you don't want to be doing these things.' It's like they wanted him to make something of himself."

Pitcher **Shayne Bennett** (1996-97) on being introduced to baseball as a 12 year old in his native Australia:
"I learned the game from a video, 'The Dodgers' Way to Play Baseball.' I was watching this and they were showing you the grip for a curveball, the grip for a slider, the grip for a changeup. That's where I learned most of the stuff."

Pitcher **Donnie Bridges** (2000-02, 2004-05) on pitching coach and longtime major leaguer **Tommy John** (2002).
"You listen to him talk every day and you learn something when he's not even trying to teach you anything. It's been great having him here, just picking his brain."

"You can learn a lot by sitting on the bench, but you learn more by playing."

Infielder **Jamey Carroll** (1998-2000, 2002)

"I'm working on the mental part of the game the most, dealing with failure. After hitting .520 every year in high school, you kind of get used to doing that. Then in my first year in the Gulf Coast League (in 1997) I was batting .235 and wondering, 'Why can't I hit? A month ago, I was the top player in high school and now I'm just another Joe.' "

Third baseman **Scott Hodges** (2000-02, 2005)

"My first batting practice (with Toronto in the late 1980s) I hit a ball over the right-field fence off Dave Stieb. The very next pitch, he hit me in the ribs. What do you do? There was no sorrow. There was no anger. It was like, 'Welcome to the big leagues.' "

Hitting coach **Rob Ducey** (2004)

Manager **Keith Bodie** (2005) after the Class AA debut of third baseman **Ryan Zimmerman** (2005), who picks up three hits, scores two runs and makes a handful of fine-to-fantastic plays at third base in an 8-6 victory over Akron on June 25, 2005 at City Island:
"I've seen some debuts in my day and this is the best I've ever seen. He had no problem with the bat. He had no problem with his approach. Everything he did was outstanding."

Ryan Zimmerman (2005) on his first day with the Senators:
"The hard part is learning everybody's name. You feel bad when you don't know them right away, but it only takes a day or two to get that done."

Longtime minor leaguer and onetime major league outfielder **Dermal Brown** (2005) on having **Ryan Zimmerman** (2005) locker next to him after the Nationals' top prospect joins the Senators:
"I can educate him on all kinds of things, but I don't know if that's good or bad."

The Senators' kids' clinics begin with manager Dave Trembley's arrival in 1987

Let the Kids Play

… or Just Leave Those Little Leaguers Alone

"Parents tend to try to mold their kids into being baseball players instead of just letting them have fun."

Outfielder **Jeremy Ware** (1999-2004)

"Kids are not going to do things perfect. Parents in Little League should know better. Some of them understand, but I've seen enough of them get on their kids, saying, 'Don't swing at this, don't swing at that. Don't do this, don't do that.' It's always these bad things coming out of their mouths, instead of something positive."

Outfielder **Noah Hall** (2000, 2003)

"There's so much pressure put on kids now. Everybody wants their child to do well, but not every kid is going to be a major league player."

Manager **Dave Machemer** (2003-04)

"Little League parents are the crabgrass in the lawn of baseball. They need to just let the kids play."

Longtime major league scout **Ben McLure** of Hummelstown

Living the Life

"**Y**ou've got to be loose, because this is a loose business. But, you know, with all the odd hours, strange eating times, long bus trips and all that I don't think I'd do it if I weren't playing baseball at the end of the day."

Pitcher **Mouse Adams** (1988-90)

Catcher **Jeff Banister** (1988-90) on getting married:

"We're used to being apart. We've actually been together maybe one and a half of the four years we've been seeing each other, but that doesn't mean I don't miss her."

"It's pretty simple: you get up, you eat, you watch TV, you go to the stadium, you play ball, you come back, you sleep. Then you do it all over again the next day."

Second baseman **Kevin Burdick** (1988-89)

KEVIN BURDICK

"We spend most of our time on the field, so we're always looking for places to eat late because the games are over late. You look for places where you can get a bite to eat after 11 o'clock."

Catcher-third baseman **Michael Barrett** (1998)

"I'm used to living out of a suitcase. I kind of like it. When I was 18, I went to college at Cal-Berkeley, so I was out of the house early. ... I made my mother really upset one day when I said being home was like being in a hotel. I didn't get dinner that night."

Infielder **Geoff Blum** (1996, 1998)

Cliff Floyd, then one of baseball's top prospects, is safe at second on this 1993 pickoff against Canton, but the Senators reach for the Mylanta after Floyd is hit in the head with the throw. The stunned Floyd survives to play 17 seasons in the majors.

M*A*S*H

Catcher **Jeff Banister** (1988-90) on the possibility of having a cancer-infected leg amputated in high school:
"I told (the doctor) I would rather die than lose my leg. I had always been an athlete, and I couldn't imagine living without my legs."

JEFF BANISTER

Catcher **Jeff Banister** (1988-90) on fracturing his neck while blocking the plate for Lee College in 1984; he eventually makes a full recovery and reaches the majors with Pittsburgh:
"I thought I was dead. I was dazed and everything seemed to go in slow motion. Even the voices around me sounded slurred."

Pitcher **Derek Aucoin** (1994-95) on giving up four runs in only two innings during his first appearance with the Senators following shoulder surgery after the 1994 season:
"I'm happy to be back. Sometimes you wonder if you're ever going to throw another pitch, if your next pitch is going to be your last. Now, I have to start bringing down my ERA. Right now, it's above the moon."

Relief pitcher **Kirk Bullinger** (1995-97) on spending five weeks rehabbing his strained right elbow at the Montreal Expos' spring training facilities in West Palm Beach, Fla.:

"A month and a week there can take its toll on you, but I did come back with a healthy tan."

Center fielder **Rondell White** (1992-93, 1996) on returning to City Island on an injury rehab assignment that starts by crushing the pitching in the neophyte Gulf Coast League:

"I felt bad about that. They're 18 year olds out of high school and I was trying to raise their ERAs over 10."

Catcher **Bob Henley** (1996-97) on the season-ending concussion he suffers in 1997:

"The strangest part is I can take batting practice and infield. I can do all of those things because they're repetitive. But when it comes to the part of the game where you need your highest level of concentration, I can't do it. I can't focus on a pitch. My brain can't tell me to react the way I need to."

Pitching coach **Brent Strom** (1998) on trying to save his career in the late 1970s with the same ligament transplant surgery revolutionized a few years earlier by Dr. Frank Jobe on **Tommy John:**

"When you win 288 games in the major leagues and it works, it's called 'Tommy John surgery.' When you win 22 games in the majors for your career and it doesn't work, then it's called 'Brent Strom surgery.' "

BRENT STROM

"The tough thing about this is that you work your whole life, you prove yourself over and over, and the door opens for you and everything is right in your grasp and then an injury takes it away from you. You try to grit it out, but cortisone doesn't help. Finally, you have to get surgery. It's tough because other guys move in and take your spot."

Catcher **Bob Henley** (1996-97) after shoulder surgery in 1999

Pitching coach **Tommy John** (2002) said of posting 164 of his 288 career victories in 14 seasons after undergoing the then-revolutionary ligament-transplant surgery that still bears his name.

"The statistic I'm most proud of is that after my surgery, I never missed a start because of my elbow."

"He's my idol. He resurrected my career."

Pitching **Brent Billingsley** (2001-02) on **Tommy John** (2002), who a quarter-century earlier undergoes experimental ligament-transplant surgery that not only saves his career but dozens of others – including that of Billingsley.

Outfielder **Jeremy Ware** (1999-2004) on his midseason laser eye surgery in 2000:

"When they're zapping it, you can smell something burning. I thought, 'Oh, well, that's cool ... that's only my eye.' "

Outfielder **Jeremy Ware** (1999-2004) on reliever **Chad Bentz** (2003-04) pitching with conjunctivitis – aka pink eye – and picking up the save in a 2003 victory over Erie on City Island:

"Oh, great, we're going to be screwed now; we all shook his hand after the game."

Manager **Dave Machemer** (2003-04) on reliever **Chad Bentz** (2003-04) pitching with conjunctivitis:

"I saw some fire in his eyes. Of course, he couldn't see out of one of those eyes."

Right-handed pitcher **Jeff McAvoy** (2002) on rehabbing his shoulder in Florida:

"I got to the point during the rehab of going out to the batting cages – you can only do so much before you get bored – and started throwing left-handed. It got to the point where I could play catch left-handed accurately from 90 feet."

Pitching coach **Tommy John** (2002) on his need for hip replacement surgery:

"Oh, it's not bad. I've only dislocated it three times in the last 13 years. That's not too bad, is it?"

Shortstop **Josh Labandeira** (2003-05) on playing through a torn labrum in his right shoulder:

"It felt fine one day and then I couldn't lift my arm the next day. The frustrating thing about this is that my arm is the best of my tools."

"I don't want anybody to be hurt, but I want to play, too."
                    Infielder **Victor Gutierrez** (2003)

Outfielder **Jeremy Ware** (1999-2004) on missing more than a week in 2004 with a strained right calf while struggling with a .180 batting average:

"It just won't get loose. It's not like I'm trying to sit on my batting average."

JOHN STEARNS

Outfielder **Dee Haynes** (2005) on spending time on the phantom DL with the St. Louis Cardinals' Class AAA affiliate in Memphis before being acquired by Washington in 2005 and assigned to Harrisburg:

"They had five outfielders there and I was the lowest-paid guy."

Manager **John Stearns** (2006, 2008-09) on his fingers, mangled by 13 seasons of catching in the majors and minors:

"Now if I'm at the bar I try to hide them. I could be out with a girl and I'm like, 'Oh, please don't look at those.' "

Infielder **Anthony Rendon** (2012-13) after fracturing his left ankle early in the 2012 season:

"The biggest challenge (in recovering) was running the bases and making left turns like in NASCAR."

ANDREW LINKER

Mayflies

One kind of pest ...

"The beverage sales definitely go down because the mayflies drop down into your drinks."
Food concession manager **Tom Kunkle** in June 1992

"Actually, they are a sign of a healthy river and a good, natural environment. We should be glad they are here, and that they are here only briefly."

General manager **Todd Vander Woude**

Pitcher **Jeff McAvoy** (2002) after leaving his car in the players' parking lot on City Island while he was rehabbing his injured right shoulder in Florida:
"The mayflies kept it company. When I got back, there was about a half-inch of mayflies just baked onto the windshield. Heavy-duty Windex took it all off."

TODD VANDER WOUDE

"About the only way we could reduce the mayfly population is by polluting the river, and that's not exactly a goal of this administration."
Harrisburg city spokesman Randy King in 1991

84

Media

... another kind of pest

" I really don't do a whole lot of talking to the media, because of the perception that there's not going to be anything positive that I'm doing. I have a good year and it goes unnoticed, but if I display anything wrong that would be a big deal."

Oft-troubled outfielder **Milton Bradley** (1999) in 2008

Outfielder **Brandon Watson** (2002-03, 2005) on being inundated with questions after making a key throw to help preserve the Nationals' 2-0 victory over San Francisco on Sept. 22, 2005.

"I'm not used to giving interviews naked."

"Half of that stuff on the Internet really isn't true, so I just try to stay away from it."

Third baseman **Ryan Zimmerman** (2005)

Manager **Dave Trembley** (1987-89) in June 2007 on being told early in the morning by the Orioles that they are waiting for an afternoon press conference to announce he was being named interim manager:

"You know how it is in this day and age with the electronic and print media ... by 10 o'clock in the morning, people were calling me."

"It's a good thing when people want to talk to you, and I know one day that probably won't be the case. So I better enjoy it while I can."

Closer **Drew Storen** (2009-10, 2012)

"People are going to write what they want to write, say what they want to say. I've got my family and friends around me, my teammates and my organization. To come to a place like this, it's like, 'Holy crap.' It's one step closer to the big leagues."

Outfielder **Bryce Harper** (2011, 2013) on his first day in Class AA

A 2003 island reunion of 1,000-win managers: Dave Trembley (left), Dave Machemer

Milestones

" I t's amazing how many players it takes to go through the system for 1,000 wins. It makes you think of all the transactions, all the bus trips."

Dave Trembley (1987-89) on his 1,000[th] victory in 2001

Manager **Dave Machemer** (2003-04) on entering the 2002 season at Class A Clinton needing only 26 victories to reach 900 in his career:

"I'll get my 900th this year, but I don't think I'll get my 1,000[th] unless they give me the 1927 Yankees."

Dave Machemer (2003-04),who is selling Oldsmobiles back home in Benton Harbor, Mich., in 1985 when Milwaukee scout Fred Beene calls the Brewers to recommend Machemer for their managerial opening at Class A Beloit:

"I owe getting back into baseball to Fred Beene. He put in a phone call for me. If it wasn't for him, I wouldn't be celebrating my 1,000[th] victory. Maybe I'd be celebrating selling my 1,000[th] car."

The most demanding day for the game's most demanding position came on April 18, 1981, when future Senators manager Dave Huppert (2002) found himself as Rochester's starting catcher in their game at Pawtucket.

Normally, a game between the Class AAA affiliates from Baltimore and Boston generated little interest.

This game, though, would turn out to be anything but normal as the game dragged into extra innings.

And dragged.

And then dragged some more.

Ten innings went by. Then 15 ... 20 ... 25 ... 30.

Behind the plate calling pitches for Rochester in each of those innings was Huppert, who would catch 31 innings and who knows how many pitches before being lifted for a pinch-hitter in the top of the 32nd.

A few minutes later, at 4:06 a.m., the game was suspended more than 8 hours after it began.

"It was freezing," Huppert said. "It was in the low 20s by the end of the game. And we were getting hungry. By the time midnight rolled around, we were starving. Then, at 3 o'clock in the morning, we're facing Bruce Hurst throwing 90 mph."

The game would resume 9 1/2 weeks later. By then

WHO KNEW?

Exactly 36 years and one month after Manny Mota became the first player selected by the Expos in the expansion draft in 1968, outfielder Brad Wilkerson (1999-2000) became the last Expo to officially appear in a game during Major League Baseball's eight-game tour of Japan. Wilkerson played in every game on the tour, going 7-for-26 with a homer.

Huppert was well-rested, but out of the game and on the bench. The interest in the game went from nominal to national, and not just because it had lasted so long. The press box at McCoy Stadium now was packed by writers who had grown bored with covering the players' strike in the majors and became curious about the game that refused to end.

"There were 400 press people then," Huppert said of the game's completion, which did not include him. "I think it would have been a big story for me if I was still in the game."

As it was, the game lasted only one more inning, the 33rd, before Pawtucket won 3-2.

"That was a waste of our time," Huppert said, "waiting 65 days for that."

Mind Games

Better known as paralysis by analysis

"**U**ntil things are going good for you, you're always thinking too much."

Third baseman **John Wehner** (1990)

"My career turned around when I stopped caring what everybody else thought about me."

Pitcher **Joey Eischen** (1993)

Pitching coach **Brent Strom** (1998) on **Jason Baker** (1998-99) and his never-ending struggle with control:

"When he thinks about his delivery, that's when he's at his worst. A lot of things tend to clutter Mr. Baker's mind. The more he thinks the worst he is. It's that way with all of us."

Manager **Rick Sweet** (1998-99) on the differences between Class A and AA:

"Double-A is more mental. You expect more from players. You're expected to hustle. You're expected to hit. You're expected to field. You don't make the same mistakes two, three or four times. If you do, you go back to Class A. Double-A is where the game takes on the look of what I call 'real baseball.' "

Pitcher **Mark Mangum** (2001-02) on abruptly retiring from the game during the 2002 season at age 23:

"When I won a game or pitched well, it didn't do anything for me. When I lost a game, I wasn't angry. After a while you realize that's not the way it's supposed to be. ... My teammates love the game, I like the game. I wish I loved it. That was hardest thing for me to discover."

"I don't think about it. I was thinking back when all of this started. It didn't get me anywhere, so I stopped thinking. It's like I have the plague. My hitting coach won't even talk to me."

Outfielder **Tommy Gregg** (1987) on starting the 1990 season in a 2-for-44 slump with the Atlanta Braves

TOMMY GREGG

"In a slump, you try to do too much to get out of it. There are so many things going through your head. The last thing you're thinking is to get a good pitch to hit. You can be the smartest hitter when you're walking to the plate, then turn into the stupidest hitter once you're in the batter's box."

Hitting coach **Troy Gingrich** (2008-11)

Third baseman **Ryan Zimmerman** (2005) on his major league debut with the Nationals on Sept. 1, 2005:

"I'm not so much nervous as I am excited. After playing the game your whole life, no matter what stage you're on, you don't get nervous. You get excited or overexcited to play, but you don't get nervous."

"It feels a lot more like a job when you're struggling than when you're doing well."

Pitcher **Chuck James** (2010)

Moments in Time

Relief pitcher **Kirk Bullinger** (1995-97) on his 20 relatives and friends in the stands at St. Louis on Sept. 26, 1998, the day he gives up Mark McGwire's 68th home run in the seventh inning of the Montreal Expos' 7-6 victory over the Cardinals:

"I think they got a bigger kick out of my giving up a home run to McGwire than if I got him out."

Catcher **Brian Schneider** (1999) on handling ceremonial first pitches for the Nationals from President George W. Bush in 2005 and Vice President Dick Cheney in 2006:

"I'm just checking them off the list. I want the Secretary of State next."

Before catching presidential first pitches, Brian Schneider was winning an EL title in '99

Outfielder **Terrmel Sledge** (2001-02) on starting the Nationals' first game on April 4, 2005 in Philadelphia:

"Playing in front of 44,000 … that was an unbelievable feeling … just a zing going through my body from head to toe."

The Kid and The Man

Shortly before his death in January 2013, Hall of Famer Stan Musial sought one more item for his trophy room. Seems The Man wanted a signed jersey from The Kid – Nationals 20-year-old out-fielder Bryce Harper (2011, 2013) who in 2012 became the youngest position player named National League rookie of the year. "I was like, '*Whoa!*' Harper told a Washington radio show after Musial died. "What a great honor."

Moneyball

"I never viewed this team as a sports-athletic project. To me, it's always been an economic development project."
Harrisburg mayor **Stephen Reed** on the Senators in 1987

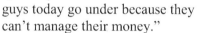

Pitching coach **Dave Tomlin** (1994), whose top salary was $106,000 during his career in the majors from 1972-86, on players' finances today:
"If you can't make a living on $3 million a year you better get another agent or financial advisor. Even with that, in 10 years there'll be some guys today go under because they can't manage their money."

Pitcher **Tommy Phelps** (1996-99) on minor league meal money:
"That $20 a day in meal money ain't nothing to eat on. When you're on the road, it's McDonald's and, 'Can I have the No. 4 combo, please?'"

Mike Berger, assistant to Montreal Expos general manager **Jim Beattie**, in 2001 on Major League Baseball's threat to fine team officials $1 million for discussing labor talks with the players' union:
"I wish I had the money to tell you what was going on."

Name Games

Team president **Scott Carter** in December 1986 on how he and owner Jerry Mileur picked the team's new name after its relocation from New Hampshire:

"In minor league baseball, there are two philosophies and they are about equally split. We are a member of the school that likes to have an independent name. We chose the 'Senators' for two reasons – one, because of the tie to the state capital and, two, because of the tradition and roots to Harrisburg."

Public address announcer **Chris Andree** on introducing New Haven center fielder Coco Crisp before his first at-bat on City Island in 2002:

"That's the first time I've ever announced a breakfast cereal at the ballpark."

Harrisburg mayor **Stephen Reed** in 2004 on selling the naming rights for RiverSide Stadium to Commerce Bank Park for $3.5 million over 15 years:

"We always had an interest in selling the naming rights. Why not? Ask most taxpayers which they would have, 'Keep the name RiverSide Stadium and you pay the $3.5 million (for ballpark upgrades) or let Commerce Bank Park exist and they pay it?' It's almost a no-brainer."

Outfielder **Dee Haynes** (2005) on joining the Senators from the St. Louis Cardinals' organization midway through the 2005 season:

"I've met everybody now. If I remember their names or not, well, that's a different story."

Shortstop **Josh Labandeira** (2003-05) on why Expos manager Frank Robinson calls him only by his first name during his time with Montreal:

"He won't call me by my last name. He told me, 'By the time I call you for a situation, the situation is going to be gone.' "

S ome of the more unique nicknames for Harrisburg's players and managers since 1890:

The Impaler with preferred weapon of choice in 1996

Bad Dude	Manager John Stearns (2006, 2008-09)
Bam Bam	Outfielder Bryce Harper (2011, 2013)
Bear	Pitcher Chad Bentz (2003-04)
Bull	Pitcher Brooks Lawrence (1951)
Bullfrog	Pitcher Bill Dietrich (1931)
Bunny	Outfielder John Roser (1930)
Caveman	Third baseman Shane Andrews (1993)
Chili World	Right fielder Wes Chamberlain (1989)
Crash	Outfielder Craig Brown (1987)
Ducky	Pitcher Johnny Tillman (1928-30)
Ee-Yah	Catcher Hughie Jennings (1890)
El Duque	Pitcher Orlando Hernandez (2010)
Foghorn	Infielder Doggie Miller (1893)
Footsie	First baseman Fernando Seguignol (1998)
Fats	Outfielder Clarence Jenkins (1924-27)
G-Whiz	Outfielder Glenn Murray (1993)
Gato	Shortstop Felix Fermin (1987)
Heavy	Outfielder Oscar Johnson (1924, 1927)
Hinkey	Outfielder Henry Haines (1933)
Hoops	Catcher Brian Schneider (1999)
The Impaler	Outfielder Vladimir Guerrero (1996)
The Legend	Pitcher-Donnie Bridges (2000-02, 2004-05)
Mouse	Pitcher Steve Adams (1988-90)
Old Reliable	First baseman Ben Taylor (1925)
Oogie	Pitcher Ugueth Urbina (1993-94)
Pop	Catcher William Schriver (1906-07)
Rabbit	Outfielder Joe Caffie (1951)
Rap	Outfielder Herbert Dixon (1922-27)
Rev	Infielder Walter Cannady (1925-27)
Rock	Outfielder Rondell White (1992-93, 1996) and coach Tim Raines Sr. (2007)
Shakespeare	Pitcher Willie Fordham (1952)
Shark	Outfielder Roger Bernadina (2007-08)
Shooter	Manager Jim Tracy (1993)
Sleepy	First baseman-outfielder Cliff Floyd (1993)
Slick Willie	Catcher John Wilson (2004-05)
Sliding Billy	Player-manager Billy Hamilton (1905-06)
Slim	Pitcher Jimmy Williams (1994)
Snake	First baseman Fred Henry (1933)
Steamer	Outfielder Jim Flanagan (1913)
Sugar	Pitcher Bob Cain (1931)
Superman	Outfielder Dee Haynes (2005)
Tootie	Shortstop Tomas de la Rosa (1999) and outfielder Clarence Myers (2001)
Wild Thing	Pitcher Jason Baker (1998-99)
Woody	Pitcher Kirk Rueter (1993)

ANDREW LINKER

No-hitters

The Real Ones and the Real Close Ones

Pitching coach **Jerry Reuss** (2000), who in 1980 no-hit San Francisco, on watching **Troy Mattes** (1999-2000, 2003) come within two outs of no-hitting Altoona on April 26, 2000 at RiverSide Stadium:
"It took me back 20 years. I remember the excitement. Every pitcher who ever goes out there should experience getting a no-hitter. That's a memory you can't erase."

Seung Song (2002-03) after throwing the first no-hitter of the Senators' modern era, beating Erie 2-1 on April 28, 2003 at RiverSide – one day after the Phillies' Kevin Millwood authors the last no-hitter at Philadelphia's Veterans Stadium:
"When I went to bed last night I was thinking about Kevin Millwood's no-hitter for the Phillies. I was thinking, 'I'm going to throw a no-hitter tomorrow.' I kept thinking about it last night. It's unbelievable."

Catcher **Scott Ackerman** (2000, 2002-03) after **Seung Song** (2002-03) no-hits Erie for seven innings in a 5-2 victory on June 1, 2003 – just five weeks after Seung no-hits Erie on City Island:
"With Song, you just sit back like you're in a recliner and chill out."

Erie manager Kevin Bradshaw on **Seung Song** (2002-03) after the right-hander holds the SeaWolves to two unearned runs on five hits in three starts and 21 innings against them in 2005:
"I'd like to sit behind home plate sometime and watch him, because our guys are coming back to the dugout and saying they have no idea how to figure him out."

Former Senator **Jason Brown** (2002-04) on catching the no-hitter thrown by Trenton's Tyler Clippard at Harrisburg on Aug. 17, 2006:
"He did everything well. I couldn't put down a wrong finger."

Number Crunching

“ **I** try not to get caught up in the stats, because I would start thinking about them going up to the plate, and I have enough to think about already when I go up there. If I start thinking about my stats, bad things are going to happen.”

Outfielder **Chris Stowers** (1997-98)

“Branch Rickey once called statistics lies and nothing but damn lies. Or they can be what agents call inducements. They'll say, 'Let's keep track of this because this is what's positive for my client, so maybe we can get him a bonus.' ”

Pitching coach **Jerry Reuss** (2000)

Manager **Dave Machemer** (2003-04) on the Senators' 52-90 finish in 2004:

“Look, we're last in the league in hitting and we're last in the league in pitching. We've given up more home runs than any other team and we've hit less than any other team. When you start looking at those things combined, where else can we be but last place?”

And the Hits Just Keep on Coming

D odgers outfielder Andre Ethier had quite the streak going in 2012 with 10 straight hits. Got himself quite a bit of national attention for it, too. The record, though, for the majors and Negro Leagues is held by another outfielder who once called City Island his home. That would be **Rap Dixon** from the all-black Harrisburg Giants from 1922-27 who in 1929 put together 14 straight hits, along with two walks for the Baltimore Black Sox. The major league record

RAP DIXON

remains 12 straight, set by Johnny Kling in 1902, and matched by Pinky Higgins in 1938 and Walt Dropo in 1952. The all-time record belongs to Reading Keystones outfielder George Quellich, who had 15 straight hits during the 1929 International League season – the same summer as Dixon's streak.

Optimism

Team president **Scott Carter** after the Senators lost their season opener in 1987:
"What it means is we can be 139-1."

Catcher **Jeff Banister** (1988-90) on simply being able to play the game after surviving cancer in high school and a fractured neck in college:
"That's the great thing about baseball: You can fail one day, but if you keep working, you can come back to succeed in another game. That's easy for me, that working every day at it. After going for months without seeing the sun at one point everything seems brighter to me."

Outfielder **Phil Dauphin** (1994-95) after the Senators lose for the 13th time in 16 games:
"We're not snake bit; we're just losing."

Pitcher **Brandon Agamennone** (1999-2002) on returning to City Island with the Bowie Baysox in 2003 and promptly giving up homers to former teammates **Glenn Davis** (2002-03) and **Jeff Bailey** (2002-03) in a 7-6 loss to the Senators:
"I've matured over the last couple of years. Two years ago, I would have been on a bridge watch after that."

KEITH BODIE

Manager **Keith Bodie** (2005) after the Senators' 0-2 start in 2005:
"We have – what? – 140 games left. We still have a chance."

Passing the Time

S mooth-pated manager and thoroughbred racing lover **Mike Quade** (1991-92) on his disdain for harness racing:

"You have a better chance of finding me in a barber shop than a harness track. I just hate those buggies."

When not exchanging pleasantries with umpires, manager Mike Quade likes to check out the ponies at Penn National during the 1991-92 seasons

"In my first couple of years in pro ball I was reading Faulkner and Steinbeck. On the bus there are so many distractions that I couldn't get into the book. I like to read every word in the sentence to see what the writer is trying to say. I was reading sentences four or five times … it was really difficult to read on the bus because we would be bumping around."

Harvard-educated pitcher **Bob Baxter** (1994)

Pitcher **Jeff McAvoy** (2002) on fishing along the Susquehanna River with teammate **Ron Chiavacci** (2001-03):

"He knows what he's doing because he thinks like a fish."

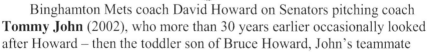

Binghamton Mets coach David Howard on Senators pitching coach **Tommy John** (2002), who more than 30 years earlier occasionally looked after Howard – then the toddler son of Bruce Howard, John's teammate with the Chicago White Sox in the mid-1960s:

"Actually, my mom told me that Tommy never really baby-sat for us; he would just come over after playing golf and tell us how he did on each hole."

Patriotism

Catcher **Jeff Banister** (1988-90) on taking part in the Eastern League's Diamond Diplomacy tour of the Soviet Union after the 1989 season:

"The Star Spangled Banner, we hear it every night at home, but to hear it there (in Russia) … well, it was the most powerful experience of my life. It made me realize how much I take for granted."

Senators batting coach **Rob Ducey** (2004) on concerns of potential terrorism at the 2004 Olympics in Athens, Greece, where he took time off during Harrisburg's season to be a designated hitter for Team Canada:

"The worry for me is embarrassing myself."

ROB DUCEY

Rob Ducey on being Canada's DH during the 2004 Olympics:

"I've played on many teams, but I really felt like I fit in better there. That was the first time I was ever on a team where you weren't looking over your shoulder. You were pulling for everybody. You had a common goal. There was not one selfish person on that team. And we had one common bond: We were Canadian."

Outfielder **Jimmy Van Ostrang** (2012-13) on helping Team Canada qualify for the 2013 World Baseball Classic:

"Everything is magnified. There are a handful of games and that's it. There aren't 140 more games to play catch up. It's now and that's it. It's baseball in its purest form. … It's 100 percent about wins and losses."

Outfielder **Jeremy Ware** (1999-2004), a native of Guelph, Ontario, in 2000 on the prospect of playing at Class AAA Ottawa:

"For once I'd be the only Canadian playing in the city and everybody else would be the foreigners."

Not unusual during the 1987-88 seasons to find Jeff King, right, alone with his thoughts

Personalities

"People think just because I'm unemotional on the field that I don't care. People who really know me know how much I care."

Third baseman **Jeff King** (1987-88)

"I look for intangibles in a player, not just his numbers. Can he do it under pressure? Is he self-motivated? Can he fit into the team concept? To me, questions like these are important."

Manager **Dave Trembley** (1987-89)

Pitcher **Joey Eischen** (1993) on his younger, wilder side:

"I can't get rid of that reputation I built up as a kid. Guys know who I am by what I did in the past. People in baseball are worse than any newspaper person or politician. They hold the bar really high for people standing right in front of them, but they never look at themselves to see what they did when they played."

Dave Trembley likes players who point themselves in the right direction

Pitching

"**I**n my second life I want to come back as a left-handed pitcher. It's the quickest way to the big leagues."

Catcher **Tom Prince** (1987)

Manager **Jim Tracy** (1993) on watching soft-tossing **Kirk Rueter** (1993) walk only seven batters in 59 2/3 innings before the left-hander's promotion to Class AAA Ottawa and, eventually, Montreal:

"There aren't too many guys who use that kind of brush to paint the plate. This kid uses one of those brushes with very thin bristles."

"With the way I pitch, I know I'm not going to blow people away. I need a defense playing behind me."

Starter **Kirk Rueter** (1993)

Left-hander **Rick DeHart** (1993, 1995-96) on the prevailing winds that blow toward left field on City Island:

"I knew it was going to be tough today when I pulled into the parking lot and saw 10 people behind the left-field fence waiting for balls during batting practice."

"I wouldn't pitch around anybody on this level. Your No. 3 and 4 hitters in college are your No. 8 and 9 hitters here."

Starter **Michael Mimbs** (1994)

Reliever **Derek Aucoin** (1994-95) on the Senators' power arms in 2005:

"Throwing 90 (mph) and straight is worth nothing. Ninety and behind in the count is worth nothing. Ninety without a second pitch is worth nothing. We all have good arms here, but we need polish."

Warren Moore on teaching the game to his son a couple of decades before **Trey Moore** (1997) leads the Senators to the Eastern League championship:

"I knew left-handers had more opportunities than right-handers. I started Trey at the age of 1. If he put the ball in his right hand, I'd take it out and put it in his left hand and make him throw that way."

Pitching coach **Brent Strom** (1998) on teaching better mechanics through biomechanics:

"I'm the first to admit it: I've screwed up a lot of pitchers in my time, but I'm not going to do that anymore."

> ## WHO KNEW?
> Twelve years before he became the Senators' pitching coach in 2000, Jerry Reuss became the first left-handed pitcher in major league history to win 200 career games without ever winning 20 games in a season.

Christian Parker (1998-99) on hitting 15 batters in 1999 to set a modern Senators franchise record:

"I'm not a head hunter. I don't throw hard enough to be labeled that."

"As relievers, the ultimate is to come in and pick each other up. As a reliever, you want to have that ball in your hands. If you don't, you have to check yourself out."

Rodney Stevenson (1997-2000)

Ruben Niebla (1998-99) in 1999 on being a left-handed reliever:

"It's a good life. It's a job that pays money for not so many innings. A third of an inning here, a third of an inning there. If I were right-handed, I'd be coaching by now."

"As long as the ball stays in the park it looks like a pop-up. I'll take all the 360-foot outs they'll give me."

Fly ball-happy reliever **Jeremy Salyers** (1999-2001)

" **A**nybody can go out with great stuff and win, but knowing how to pitch when you don't have your best stuff and winning, that's smart pitching."

Pitching coach **Wayne Rosenthal** (1999)

"In Double-A, if you can't change speeds and you can't get the ball below the belt you're going to get hit hard. You might get through one time in the order, but not the second and third time."

Manager **Dave Huppert** (2002)

"It's a lot easier to pitch with a lead. It's less stressful to pitch out there. Not that I'm super-stressed when it's 0-0, but it's a lot easier to pitch when there's a lead."

Starter **Cliff Lee** (2002)

"I've been there where I couldn't throw strikes. (White Sox manager) Al Lopez came to the mound one time and said to me – and it's probably the best thing he ever said to me – 'Kid, if you're going to be wild, be wild with all of your pitches. Maybe one of them will be a strike.' "

Pitching coach **Tommy John** (2002)

> **RE-BUILT TO WIN**
>
> Tommy John won 124 games in the majors in 12 seasons prior to his breakthrough arm surgery in 1974 before winning 164 in 16 seasons after the ligament transplant procedure that still bears his name.

Tommy John (2002) after becoming the pitching coach at Class AAA Edmonton in 2003 and discovering that summer daylight lasts longer there than in Harrisburg:

"I'm trying to get my pitchers to work fast and pitch quick games, so I can get nine holes of golf in."

Pitching coach **Charlie Corbell** (2003) on his staff's early season struggles as the Senators' team ERA jumps from 3.22 to 4.48 runs per game in less than a month:

"You don't have to tell me about it; I watch it every day."

"The only way to go deep into games is to get guys out early. I want to keep my team in the dugout. Nobody really thinks about time of possession in baseball, but you want to keep the opponent on the field as long as possible."

Starter **Bobby Brownlie** (2008)

"Command is the most impressive pitch."

Pitching coach **Paul Menhart** (2012-13)

Promotional Nights

VLADIMIR GORILLA

General manager **Todd Vander Woude** on the team's Star Trek promotion in 1998:

"We'll judge the best look-a-likes with the winners getting a Star Trek movie ... and we'll give you $10,000 if you can teleport yourself."

Outfielder **Jeremy Ware** (1999-2004) on wearing wool-like uniforms for a 2003 game honoring the old Harrisburg Giants of the 1920s:

"I like it warm, but playing in 96 degrees in these uniforms ... look at my hat. That's sweat dripping off of it, and I didn't put any water on it."

The Senators' poorly conceived "Vladimir Gorilla" bobblehead giveaway in 2003 is scrapped at the last minute as agents for the real Vladimir Guerrero object to their client being depicted as a primate.

Replacement Parts

S pring training 1995 was a stranger, more vexing time than normal for fringe players in the minor leagues, the ones who were not yet – or never would be – on a major league team's 40-man roster.

This was a time when major league owners, tired of their striking, non-playing players, came up with this notion of using "replacement players."

To get these players, owners preyed upon the aforementioned tweener players, outwardly promising them they would open the season in the majors and subtly suggesting that not playing along – no pun intended – with the owners in this negotiating tactic to break the union meant a good chance of never playing again in organized ball.

"The players' association asks me to support them, (but) management is telling us we have to play in the exhibition games," Expos utility player F.P. Santangelo, an infielder with the 1991 Senators, said at the time.

"It's really confusing. This isn't my battle," Santangelo said, "but I'm right in the middle of the firing line."

Santangelo ended up briefly walking out of camp that spring. He ended up spending all or parts of the next seven seasons in the majors with Montreal, San Francisco, Los Angeles and Oakland.

Countless others, like Santangelo, were forced to make the same choice. Unlike Santangelo, most of them never reached the majors, let alone last there as long as Santangelo did from 1995-2001.

"I just want the opportunity to play. Whatever decision I make I have to live with. I can't worry all my life what other people think of me. If I did that, I couldn't survive."

Outfielder **Tyrone Woods** (1992-94)

"You don't know if you're ever going to make it up there and life's too short to wait around. I wouldn't do it to take anybody's job or do it for the union or do it for the owners. It's just the situation I'm in; I have a family to support."

Pitcher **Rick DeHart** (1993, 1995-96)

F.P. Santangelo (1991) would spend all or parts of seven seasons in the majors

"I've always been in the wrong place at the wrong time. Maybe now this will be the right place at the right time. I still play the game because I love the game but, sure, it's for the money also. The money from six or seven years in the minors isn't a whole lot. This is a chance to make some money and get a start in life."

Outfielder **Marc Griffin** (1993-94)

"I don't want to cross a picket line, but that's a lot of money. That gives someone a good start in life. This might be my only shot at playing in the big leagues."

First baseman **Randy Wilstead** (1993-94) in spring 1995

"If I were one of them, I'd do it, too. I'd play this out as long as I can. They can make $30,000 in one day if they make the team."

Outfielder **Phil Dauphin** (1994-95)

"When I get there, I want to play against the guys I know from watching on television. I don't want to do it against an insurance salesman from California."

Phil Dauphin on rejecting the chance to be a replacement player

"For my family, this is what I'm in the game for all these years, but you want to make it to the majors the right way."

Pitcher **Darrin Winston** (1993-94), who would reach the majors in 1997

Road Warriors

Outfielder **Joe Munson** (1925) on traveling during his one and only season in Harrisburg:
"We traveled in two or three Cadillacs. There was this one driver, our catcher Ed Tickey, who'd scare us to death. He'd do 70 or 75 miles an hour, and one time he just missed a turn and drove right up into somebody's yard. Those were what you called real road trips."

"Just getting out of the hotel is important. You get cabin fever staying in those rooms.'
Infielder **Tommy Shields** (1988-89)

Manager **Pat Kelly** (1995-96) on the Senators' arrival from spring training in 1995 on a turbulence-filled flight that originated in West Palm Beach:

"That's as scared as I've been in a while. I thought the pilot did a helluva job, because we landed."

Pitcher **Rick DeHart** (1993, 1995-96) on surviving the same flight:
"I didn't think we were going to make it. We were landing sideways."

PAT KELLY

Manager **Rick Sofield** (1997) on his impromptu pep talk to pitcher **Mike Thurman** (1996-97, 2000) during the bumpier-than-normal, knuckleball-like airplane ride to Harrisburg before Opening Day in 1997:
"I told Thurman, 'If this isn't enough motivation to get you to (Class AAA) Ottawa so you never have to take this flight again, then nothing ever will be.' "

THREE OF A KIND
In 2013, outfielder Brian Goodwin (2012-13) joined born-DH Matt Stairs (1991) and outfielder Rondell White (1992-93, 1996) as the only Senators in modern-franchise history to post a quadruple-double with double figures in doubles, triples, homers and steals.

The 2000 Senators decide to see how many bodies they can cram into the under-sized manager's office in Reading. Somehow, they squeeze 20 players and coaches into a room barely large enough to accommodate manager Doug Sisson, pitching coach Jerry Reuss and hitting coach Tony Barbone.

Infielder **Geoff Blum** (1996, 1998) after the Senators finish the 1998 regular season with 15 of 17 games on the road.

"After being on that bus for 40 hours over the last week and a half, I forgot what life looked like. Everything to me was whatever was two rows in front of me."

Catcher-third baseman **Michael Barrett** (1998) on the same extended road trip to end the '98 season:

"We live on the bus. I'm going to write down my address as, 'Wolf's Bus, in care of (driver) Art Mattingly, Seat 3, left.' "

Roster Moves

Manager **Jim Tracy** (1993) on delivering good news and bad news to **Joey Eischen** (1993) after the pitcher ducks out early from the ballpark during a 10-9 loss to Bowie:

"We tracked him down at the Progress Grille, brought him back to the ballpark and fined him – and then we sent him to Triple-A."

Manager **Jim Tracy** (1993) on the two-level demotion of first baseman **Derrick White** (1992-93) from the Expos to Harrisburg:

"To come back from the major leagues to Double-A, that hits you like a bowl of hot peppers. They just sit there in the stomach for a while."

Manager **Rick Sofield** (1997) on the Expos' plans to add a player to his roster:

"I'm waiting for the phone to ring. If they send a guy who's 6-4, switch-hits and runs to first base in 3.9 seconds, I'll put him in the lineup right away."

Run, Labby, Run

Shortstop **Josh Labandeira** (2003-05) on why he sprints from the on-deck circle to home plate for his at-bats:

"I know certain guys just don't like it. They don't think it's the right way to play the game, but I'm sorry I have a lot of energy when I get out on the field."

Expos old-school, no-nonsense manager **Frank Robinson** giving his endorsement of Josh Labandeira's ritualistic dash to the plate:

"It's all right to run from the dugout to home plate. Now, I don't like a player who's afraid and runs from home plate back to the dugout."

Running the Show

"**W**e won't have a chicken for a mascot ... we want people to know that Harrisburg has a professional team and we want to promote it in a professional manner."
Team president **Scott Carter** in December 1986

"I actually thought for years that until Whitey Herzog got the job that I was the best general manager the St. Louis Cardinals could hire. Between Branch Rickey and Whitey Herzog, I had no doubts about that."
Senators owner and longtime St. Louis fan **Jerry Mileur**

"It's a cutthroat business. Baseball politics eclipse anything you'll see on Capitol Hill in Harrisburg, and I've done both."

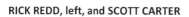

RICK REDD, left, and SCOTT CARTER

Harrisburg mayor and onetime state representative **Stephen Reed**

"Ten years ago, a minor league team was a little mom-and-pop operation, but now we've seen that if the franchise is run right we can actually make some money at it."
General manager **Rick Redd** in August 1989

"Would the city prefer not to be the owner? Absolutely. We became the proud owner of a Double-A franchise as, frankly, the last resort to otherwise seeing the team wind up in Springfield."
Harrisburg mayor **Stephen Reed**

Sisson: Unplugged

FACT: Doug Sisson verbally firebombs the media on his way out of Harrisburg following his abrupt, albeit brief, resignation as the Senators' manager in July 1999.

FICTION: The media, in return, despises Sisson.

TRUTH BE KNOWN: Sisson is a beat writer's best friend, forever filling a reporter's notepad with comments that are as candid as they are, on occasion, incendiary. The subject matter didn't matter.

DOUG SISSON

Sisson's candor often was not well-received by the Montreal Expos, who had promoted him from Class A to manage the Senators in 1999. What followed was a dizzying season in which Sisson stunningly quit on July 5 to become an assistant coach at the University of Georgia; drove 665 miles from Harrisburg to Athens, Ga., only to realize he didn't want a college job after all; successfully pleaded with his former – and irritated – employers for a second chance on City Island; rallied the Senators to an unprecedented fourth straight Eastern League title and returned them to the playoffs in 2000 only to be fired after that season for what Expos general manager Jim Beattie called "insubordination."

"This isn't Little League," Sisson said during his first summer in Harrisburg. "It's not my job to make sure everybody plays five innings a week and everybody gets to pitch and everybody goes out for Sno-Cones after the game. This is professional baseball."

On career choices: "That's what makes this such a great career. You leave the house in the morning and you never know what's going to happen that night. It's a 50-50 chance you may go home a winner or go home a loser. If we all wanted certainty, we'd have a 9-to-5 job."

On switching uniform numbers from 11 to 7 to honor then 22-month-old daughter, Tori, whose birthday is July 7:

"I asked my daughter about it and she said, 'Daddy, it's OK' ... actually, she only said, 'Daa-dee,' but I understood what she meant."

On holiday shopping for his wife, Crickett:
"The best thing about getting the Harrisburg job is that it gave me some ideas of what to get my wife for Christmas. I got her a coat, a scarf and some gloves. She's excited to go to Harrisburg so she can wear the clothes. I'm excited to go to Harrisburg for other reasons."

On having only eight healthy position players and a DH available for a doubleheader against Trenton in June 1999:
"All we need is nine. It's like the old saying, 'Don't tell me how rocky the sea is, just bring the damn ship in.' "

On developing players:
"We tell these kids every day, 'We're trying to develop good major league players, not good Double-A or Triple-A players.' "

On missed opportunities:
"Each day is a new day. If you get caught up with what you haven't done, then you start to press. And we want to avoid that."

On expectations of others before the 1999 season:
"You're expected to win in Harrisburg and I think that's neat, because you usually don't get that in minor league baseball. In a lot of minor league towns, people just go out to a game to have a night out with their family. You enjoy the game, win or lose, and go home. In Harrisburg, you go home mad if you lose and happy if you win."

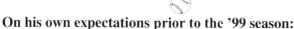

On his own expectations prior to the '99 season:
"I want to win a championship for selfish reasons. If we make it four years in a row, I want my ring to say, '1999.' If we win it, I'm not going to be on the field with a microphone saying, 'It's great to carry on the tradition of Pat Kelly, Rick Sofield and Rick Sweet.' I could care less about that. I want our team to be the best of them. Look, there have been some great teams in Harrisburg. Let's see if we can win more games than Jim Tracy's team did in 1993. I want them to be talking years from now about the '99 club. Maybe then they'll quit talking about Jim Tracy's club."

On the fans:
"In a community as passionate about baseball as Harrisburg, you have to manage with blinders on."

More on the fans:
"If those people think that their lives are more affected by our wins and losses than our lives are, then they're seriously screwed up. This is our life; that is their event for the night. ... That's why fan is short for fanatic."

To the local media after his sudden resignation on July 5, 1999 to take a job as an assistant coach at the University of Georgia:
"I'm so tired of the negativity. I'm not a negative person. I'm tired of reading it. I'm the only person in this town who cares about these players."

Expos player-development director **Donnie Reynolds** after Sisson pleads to return to the Senators a week after quitting the team and lambasting both the fans and media on his way out of Harrisburg:
"Doug's going to have to face the music there. He's going to have to do a lot of things to mend a lot of bridges. It's like he walked across the bridges, burned them and then threw a Molotov cocktail on them."

On returning to the Senators, but not first without a mea culpa:
"I was quoted correctly, but I didn't mean what I said. It was said in the heat of battle, but even then I should have known better. I have a master's degree in mass communications."

On losing:
"You can lose, but you don't ever want to act like a loser."

After falling to Reading in the 2000 Eastern League semifinals and missing a chance for a fifth straight title:
"As badly as we wanted to win another one you can't guarantee them. You can't predict them. You can't wish them upon yourself."

On trying to find a job in the independent leagues for onetime Senators outfielder Carlos Adolfo (1998-99):

"It's the least I could do for someone who has put up with me for the better part of five seasons."

On calling for a rare team meeting only minutes before an 8-6 loss at Altoona in August 2000:

"I guess I won't be making any $10,000 speeches anytime soon like Lou Holtz does."

On statistics:

"I don't know if it evens out, but if a guy hits .210 over the whole year, he's probably not a real good hitter. If he hits .330 over a whole year, he probably is. It's tough to discount the real poor statistics and the real good ones."

On Harrisburg's dominance of Reading in the 1990s:

"Other than a bad horoscope, I have no idea of how to explain it."

On rivalries:

"I hope there's no love lost between us and anybody. I want everybody to hate us. Bad teams don't have rivalries."

On his players being nervous with Expos general manager Jim Beattie watching from the grandstands:

"Sure there are going to be butterflies, but this game is all about turning that into positive energy. If it ever affects you in a negative manner, you're probably not cut out to play at a higher level in front of bigger crowds."

On the mental side of the game:

"They say baseball is 90-percent mental, but you can't bring a bunch of rocket scientists out here to win baseball games. They're pretty smart, but I like my chances against a bunch of rocket scientists."

Size Matters

U ndersized pitcher **Randy Tomlin** (1989-90) on RiverSide Stadium's cramped clubhouses, which seemingly were designed by jockeys to be used by jockeys:

"Smaller was better at that time, because I could squeeze in and out of there."

"I've pitched against Frank Thomas, so anybody after him just doesn't really look that big."

Pitcher **Michael Mimbs** (1994)

Montreal Expos manager **Frank Robinson** after seeing **Anthony Ferrari** (2002-05) – all of 5-foot-9 – work a scoreless inning against Texas in his major league debut on June 7, 2003:

"I thought it was the winning jockey at the Belmont throwing out the first pitch."

ANTHONY FERRARI

Shortstop **Josh Labandeira** (2003-05), who at 5-foot-7 personified the meaning of "short" in shortstop:

"It took me five years to get drafted. The first four years, it was always, 'You're too small.' It's a bad stereotype. It's not how big you are but how big you play the game."

Manager **John Stearns** (2006, 2008-09) in 2006 on playing today in the major leagues as the 188-pound catcher he was during his All-Star career from 1974-1984:

"I'd be a midget out there today."

Spring Draining

There are two guarantees in spring training: Players can't wait to get there and, after enough time, players can't wait to get out of there.

"After a while this gets old," said infielder **Matt Rundels** (1993-95). "When you feel physically ready to play, you want to leave."

"We're anxious to get going ... but I don't know how anxious I am to go because all we hear is that the field in Harrisburg is under water."
First baseman **Randy Wilstead** (1993-94) in March 1994

"I want to get to Harrisburg for two reasons: One, to get into the season because spring training is too long and, two, to see my family."
Manager **Dave Jauss** (1994)

Sinker-happy reliever **Kirk Bullinger** (1995-97) on giving up high-bouncing singles on the dry, rock-hard fields used in Lantana, Fla., by the Expos' minor leaguers:
"Pitching here is like pitching on I-95."

SHAYNE BENNETT

Pitcher **Shayne Bennett** (1996-97) on Lantana's fields:
"They could drop a nuclear bomb on this place and I'd be happy."

"I'm ready for some fan support. I'm tired of the 10-inning spring training games and of seeing a different pitcher every at-bat."
First baseman-outfielder **Talmadge Nunnari** (1999-2001, 2003)

Washington general manager **Jim Bowden** in December 2004 on spending his first winter in bucolic Viera, Fla., home for the Nationals' first spring training in 2005:
"It's not bad. At night, I go tip the cows over."

Strategies

"**G**et 'em on, get 'em over, get 'em in."

Manager **Dave Trembley** (1987-89)

"It's really not you; it's the players who make you. All you do is put up the lineup card."

Manager **Marc Bombard** (1990)

MARC BOMBARD

"I love National League baseball, which is pitching, running and defense. I love the moves you make in the National League. I love watching Felipe Alou outmanage somebody. I love watching Jim Leyland outmanage somebody. I love a manager having an impact, and he does in a 1-0 game."

Manager **Dave Jauss** (1994)

"If you analyze the great managers of all-time, there are a lot of hugs and there are a lot of tables being turned over."

Manager **Rick Sofield** (1997)

Manager **Dave Huppert** (2002) on moving top prospect **Brandon Phillips** (2001-02) from batting second to cleanup:

"There's not always a method to my madness. Sometimes I come in here to do the lineup and my pencil just goes that way."

Pitching coach **Randy Tomlin** (2010-11) on motivating players:

"You have to remind them every day to take advantage of where they're at. You have to tell them, 'As long as you have that uniform on, you can still play. Come to the ballpark every day thinking of that and being prepared.' "

Talkin' Basebrrr

"**Y**ou can't let little things like that bother you. You just have to believe you're playing in 85 degrees. Let the weather bother you and it will have an effect on your game."
Infielder and native Californian **F.P. Santangelo** (1991) on opening the 1991 season playing with wind-chill temperatures in the 20s on City Island.

Advice from outgoing manager **Jim Tracy** (1993) to incoming manager **Dave Jauss** (1994):
"The only advice I'd tell him is to make sure he has a warm coat in April and, depending on what the Susquehanna River decides to do before opening night, make sure you have Totes to put over your spikes."

Manager **Rick Sofield** (1997) on playing April baseball in the Eastern League, where City Island is among the southernmost cities:
"It doesn't make any difference with the southernmost club to the northernmost club. We're all freezing our asses off everywhere we go."

Outfielder and native of Guelph, Ontario, **Jeremy Ware** (1999-2005) on playing in the cold that usually accompanies the first month of the Eastern League season:
"Hey, we're not stupid up there; we come in when it's cold. Everybody's saying to me, 'Hey, you're from Canada, you're used to this.' Yeah, but I've been in Florida (for spring training) with you guys, too. I've been climatized, but then I was traumatized coming back here for another season."

"I'm a Michigan boy. I'm no fool. I grew up in that weather. I have my long-johns with me. Always."
Manager **Dave Machemer** (2003-04)

Long sleeves are the norm in April, as they are here for the Senators' 1989 home opener

Hitting coach **Tony Barbone** (2000) on standing too close to the dugout heater on April 8, 2000 in Altoona, where game-time temperature with wind chill is 15 degrees:

"My pants were stuck to my socks. They were melted onto them."

First baseman-outfielder **Talmadge Nunnari** (1999-2001, 2003) after a 9-8 loss on April 9, 2000 in Altoona, where the game begins with a wind chill of 10 degrees and ends in snow:

"That was Penn State football weather out there. I've never played in anything that cold in my life. I don't think anybody on this team has – even Ware, and he's from Canada."

Infielder **Scott Zech** (1999-2001) on his preference to opening the season as a utility player in Harrisburg or being an everyday player in the balmy, Class A Florida State League:

"It's a no-brainer. I'd rather be up here freezing my butt off."

"I know it's a cliché, but it's going to be cold for the other team, too."
Pitcher **Jeff Andrews** (2001)

"I've played in weather worse than this in college (at Southwest Missouri State). We started playing there in January. There were times you were shoveling snow off the field just to play."
Outfielder **Matt Cepicky** (2001-02)

First baseman-outfielder **Terrmel Sledge** (2001-02) on preparing to play at Class AAA Edmonton:
"I'm going to pack my long johns, my ski mask, my overalls and I'll be ready to go."

Manager **Keith Bodie** (2005) after traveling from his Arizona home with his wife, Stacy, to find themselves navigating through snow-covered Harrisburg in the winter of 2005:
"Somebody asked me what my first thought of Harrisburg was. Well, my first thought was how an aircraft going 150 miles an hour was going to stop on a snowy runway? It was like, 'Oh, man.' … We're glad the snow stopped. We were worried that we may not see our children again."

California-born pitcher **Stephen Strasburg** (2010-11) on preparing to make his City Island debut only to have it delayed by rain, lightning and a power outage:
"It's hard, especially when you go out there and get mentally ready, and then they say there's a delay. But that's part of pitching up here in Pennsylvania. You're just not going to have that perfect weather like you do in Cali."

Former Senators manager **Dave Trembley** (1987-89) after joining the Baltimore Orioles' major league coaching staff in 2007:
"I spent two years managing in [Triple-A] Ottawa. When the weather was in the 20s, all the players complained about it. We were at Yankee Stadium and it was snowing, but I didn't hear players complain about it, because they were in the big leagues."

Teaching Moments

" I'm a firm believer that the best way to develop players is to win, creating a positive environment. In addition to that, I'm a terribly hard loser."

Manager **Marc Bombard** (1990)

"The future, I've learned in this game, is today and I work for today."

Manager **Jim Tracy** (1993)

"To a certain extent, fans are not cognizant of why we're here. Some of them think all you're here for is to win. I want to win, too, but what's vitally important for the organization is that I'm a teacher first. ... Preparing them to go up is bigger than the won-loss record."

Manager **Jim Tracy** (1993)

Manager **Jim Tracy** (1993) on his talk with the Senators prior to beating Albany-Colonie 8-4 in the fourth and final game of the rain-interrupted, sometimes sloppy 1993 Eastern League semifinals:

"It was very brief. I prefaced it by telling them this is no time for me to stand up and do my best Dale Carnegie. I just wanted to get them refocused."

First baseman **Randy Wilstead** (1993-94) on manager **Pat Kelly** (1995-96):

"He's a very easy guy ... if you don't push the wrong buttons. If you do push the wrong buttons, he can put the fear of God into you."

"Discipline is a big part of baseball, but not to the point where you can't enjoy yourself on the field. Part of the learning process is learning to obey, but I don't crack a whip or anything like that."

Manager **Pat Kelly** (1995-96)

Senators manager Marc Bombard delivers a teaching
moment for an umpire during the 1990 season

"I always tell them I hit .286 in the majors. I just never tell them how many at-bats I had there."
Pat Kelly
on his seven career at-bats in the majors

"I will not sacrifice development for winning. It's an impossible thing to sell to the fans, but I'm going to develop a guy like Mike Thurman first before I'm going to satisfy somebody in Section G."
Rick Sofield

Manager **Rick Sweet** (1998-99) on why he prefers non-starting players to coach at first base:
"There are things I want them to do down there … it's not a show-up-and-check-out-the-women kind of thing."

"I'm big on developing winning players and you do that by winning in the minors. Now, you don't have to win the whole thing, but you need to be competitive to the point where you're in the hunt right down to the end. That's when you find out what kind of players you have."
Manager **Rick Sweet** (1998-99)

121

"You always have a curfew, but their time away from the ballpark is their time. It's like any parent would say to a kid, 'Don't do anything stupid. Don't put yourself in a bad position.' They have to remember they are representing more than themselves, that they are representing an organization. I've been in some cities where we had to put some bars off limits, but in Harrisburg we don't have to do that. That's a compliment to the city."

Manager **Rick Sweet** (1998-99)

Manager **Doug Sisson** (1999-2000) on the early season struggles of former major league pitcher **Roberto Duran** (1999):

"He was going to throw a minimum number of pitches and a maximum number of pitches. Our job is to run guys out there and let them develop. If we lose 11-0 but he learns something from it, then we've done our jobs."

Pitching coach and former National League All-Star **Jerry Reuss** (2000) on keeping his ideas fresh for prospects, even if his stories are old:

"I keep telling them the same stuff. But I change teams every three years so it's always like trying on a new wardrobe, isn't it?"

"Players today are different, but that's not a surprise. Every generation is new. They want to make their presence felt. It seems that unless you have some numbers behind you, players today will say, 'What have you ever done?' Well, they can read the back of my baseball card."

Pitching coach **Jerry Reuss** (2000)

"Guys are curious about your career, but it just wasn't relevant to them. Guys today are more concerned about their careers than they are about yours."

Pitching coach **Jerry Reuss** (2000)

"A coach can only impart knowledge; he cannot impart talent."

Pitching coach **Tommy John** (2002)

"One of the things I have found is that good coaches can suggest things in many different ways. You may have to say it five different ways and it's like you're talking Mandarin Chinese, but then you'll say something and they'll say, 'Oh, OK, I see what you're saying.' That's the whole secret of teaching, whether it's golf or baseball."

Pitching coach **Tommy John** (2002)

Pitching coach **Tommy John** on why he made only one mid-inning visit to the mound in his first 40 games with the Senators in 2002:

"I saw Dave Righetti one night have a no-hitter going (for the Yankees), but every inning the pitching coach would come out and give him a pitching lesson. He was throwing a no-hitter and they were telling him, 'Try this, try that.' You can't do that in the middle of a ballgame. You just make a note and work on that problem later. You can't give a lesson on the mound in 30 seconds."

"I want to win but, in the same breath, in the minor leagues you want to develop players to go the next level. And I believe you can develop as you win. It breeds confidence when you win."

Manager **Dave Machemer** (2003-04)

"Just because you were able to play the game doesn't mean you're able to teach the game. Some of the best coaches never had the opportunity to play at the major league level."

Hitting coach and longtime major leaguer **Rob Ducey** (2004)

Hitting coach **Eric Fox** (2001, 2012-13) on facing opposing players he once coached:

"You want them to do well, but it's a Catch-22 because you also want to win."

Pitching coach **Randy Tomlin** (2009-11) on being a quiet talker:
"I figure people listen better when you whisper."

The master of the knuckleball, left-hander Rich Sauveur, and the master of handling it, catcher Tom Prince, walk from the bullpen to the dugout before winning the pivotal Game 3 of the 1987 finals against Vermont on City Island

Tools of the Trade

"I used a bat that weighed 39 ounces in the spring and one that weighed 37 in the summer. These guys today use 30-ounce bats and they think they're heavy."

Senators outfielder **Joe Munson** (1925), the Eastern League's first Triple Crown winner and its last .400 hitter, in 1987

Pitcher **Rich Sauveur** (1987) on his knuckleball:

"I just file my fingernails the day before I pitch, throw it at the catcher's mask and hope it drops in."

Tom Prince (1987) on catching Sauveur's knuckleball:

"As a catcher, you just try to snatch it when you think it's done doing whatever it's going to do."

Trade Winds

Shortstop **Felix Fermin** (1987) in April 1992 waiting for a trade from the Cleveland Indians, who eventually deal him – and his $1 million salary – to Seattle for shortstop Omar Vizquel:

"When you make the good money and they don't play you, they have to do something. I know I can go somewhere and play. Right now, I collect my check every two weeks and put it in the bank. You know, security."

Pitcher **Justin Wayne** (2001-02) on being traded in 2002 from the contraction-threatened Expos to the Florida Marlins:

"At least I'm going to a team that's still in business."

Pitching coach **Tommy John** (2002) on Wayne's trade to Florida:
"I hate to lose him. He got my humor. Not everybody gets it."

Pitching coach **Tommy John** (2002) on the plethora of moves by Montreal in 2002 that creates a constant turnover of Harrisburg's roster in Class AA:

"That's why I've been throwing higher up on the hill during batting practice … just in case they want to activate me."

First baseman **Larry Broadway** (2003-05) on being on a golf course in Florida when learning in December 2003 that the Expos had blocked his path to the majors by trading for Yankees first baseman Nick Johnson:

"That just ruined the rest of my golf game. Not that it was any good in the first place."

Manager **Dave Machemer** (2003-04) in mid-April 2003 on the pending arrival of visa-delayed outfielder **Jeremy Ware** (1999-2004) from Canada:

"We'll look for a sighting in the next three to four days. He's going to be flying in with the geese."

Trouble at Home

In the summer of '94, and after two failed attempts to unload his team, Jerry Mileur reached an agreement to sell the Senators for $4.1 million to a quartet of investors from suburban Philadelphia.

In the fall of '94, one of the new owners, Steven Resnick, proclaimed that he was looking forward to maximizing Harrisburg's market.

Then Resnick and his partners, who included Reading Phillies owner Craig Stein, clandestinely tried to move the team – first to the Lehigh Valley and then to Springfield, Mass.

What followed was a protracted war of words between the Gang of Four from Philly and Harrisburg mayor Stephen Reed, who was determined to keep the Senators from moving and, gasp, face the prospect of not having a team play on his beloved City Island.

"I'm going to have to smack him on the nose," Reed said of Stein.

Reed didn't have to.

The National Association, the governing body of minor league baseball, did that for him by forcing the Gang of Four in the summer of '95 to negotiate a new deal to sell the Senators to the city of Harrisburg for $6.7 million, then a record sum for a Class AA franchise.

Team owner **Jerry Mileur** on his aborted attempts to sell the Senators before finally finding a taker in Stein, Resnick and Co. for $4.1 million:

"These deals are like those Saturday serials, 'The Perils of Pauline' … except she always survived. My deals always died. Every week she gets tied up on the train trestle but always gets off. Every week we've hung on to the trestle and fallen off."

Senators general manager **Todd Vander Woude** on having to handle a parade of television interviews after the Senators' owners announce early in the 1995 season that they plan to move the franchise to Massachusetts:

"I wish I would have known this was going to happen today, because I didn't bring a tie."

Former Eastern League president **Charles Eshbach** on the plans of the Senators' new owners in 1995 to move the franchise to Springfield:

"The new owners came in and bought the team basically with the understanding they were going to leave it in Harrisburg. Apparently, they wanted to move it from Day One. ... They gave reasons, but I don't know if I buy any of them. I think Harrisburg has more than supported its team. This is a real black eye on the Eastern League."

New Britain owner **Joe Buzas** on the closed-door league meeting in Harrisburg to determine the Senators' fate:

"We're under orders not to say anything about the meeting. Personally, I thought it was all horseshit."

Harrisburg mayor **Stephen Reed** on fans' plans to boycott the Senators after their planned move to Massachusetts is announced May 10, 1995:

"I understand the sentiment completely. I share that sentiment. But, if you enjoy baseball and you want to see young, rising stars then still come. Why should fans, because they are annoyed at Steve Resnick or Craig Stein, decide not to see baseball? You can still be mad at those guys and still come to baseball games. I will ... and I'm still mad at them."

Harrisburg mayor **Stephen Reed** to the media in May 1995 as he attempts a last-minute – and ultimately successful – attempt to keep the Senators from moving:

"If you guys interfere with me today, I'll kill you."

Harrisburg mayor **Stephen Reed** on being a de facto owner of a baseball team:

"I want to keep baseball out of City Hall and out of the day-to-day operations of government. It is a bad mix."

Local attorney **Corky Goldstein** at a roast for Harrisburg mayor **Stephen Reed** after the city of Harrisburg spends $6.7 million to buy the Senators:

"No one can call Mayor Reed a cheap politician; he's cost the city a fortune."

Tweets and Texts

Taxing the patience of management

" **I**t's a whole new team bus now. Everybody has a cell phone or a laptop. It's the information age. These guys know stuff before we do, like with player moves. They'll see it on a web page."

Manager **Doug Sisson** (1999-2000)

DOUG HARRIS

"I love giving people an inside look. Everything is an open door these days anyway, so I might as well give it to them straight from the horse's mouth. ... (But) the clubhouse is off limits. The clubhouse is our house. We're a family out here, and (the organization is) very adamant about not tweeting or writing about what goes on in the clubhouse."

Pitcher **Ryan Tatusko** (2010-13)

"It's not my cup of tea. I don't do Facebook. I don't twit or tweet, or whatever it is. I like my privacy, but to each his own. I get it, but it's just not my thing."

Nationals farm director **Doug Harris**

"We do have people who monitor this stuff on a fairly regular basis. Our position is the information you share has limits. (The players) know these limits. They know they have to watch what they say, that we expect them to adhere to the rules or there will be consequences."

Nationals farm director **Doug Harris**

"I can text, but I prefer to hear a voice."

Manager **Tony Beasley** (2011)

Vlad the Impaler

What Other Folks Had to Say About Guerrero

VLADIMIR GUERRERO

"There's not a thing he can't do exceptionally well. The thing I like about Vladimir Guerrero is that he can hit some bad pitches for hits. He can hit the pitcher's pitch."
Reading Phillies manager **Bill Robinson** in 1996

"Vladimir Guerrero may not make anyone forget Roberto Clemente, but he may make a lot of people remember him."
Trenton photographer **Dave Schofield** in 1996

"They have Superman leading the way. He has a cape underneath that uniform."
Trenton DH and onetime Senator **Tyrone Woods** (1992-94)

"This is what Babe Ruth must have looked like."
Marlins manager **John Boles** in 2000

"Guerrero's not like anybody I've ever seen. If you get the ball close to him, he's going to get the barrel of the bat to it, and his ability to keep the ball fair is unbelievable. He's one of those special guys to come along once every so many years."
Cleveland Indians manager **Eric Wedge** in 2006

Teammates mob Senators relief pitcher Jake Benz (33) after he records the final out of the 1997 Eastern League finals

Winning ...

"**B**aseball isn't exactly a game where the team that plays better wins. It's a matter of doing the right things at the right time."

Outfielder **Rick Hirtensteiner** (1992)

"I've always divided a season into thirds. It takes you the first third to get everything into place. How you play in the second third is going to be indicative as to whether you are in it or not. If you are, the last third is easy. You finish the deal then."

Manager **Rick Sofield** (1997)

"It's more important how we play than who we play."
Infielder **Izzy Alcantara** (1995-97) before the 1997 EL playoffs

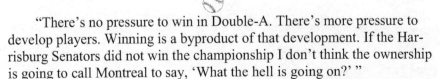

"There's no pressure to win in Double-A. There's more pressure to develop players. Winning is a byproduct of that development. If the Harrisburg Senators did not win the championship I don't think the ownership is going to call Montreal to say, 'What the hell is going on?' "

Manager **Rick Sweet** (1998-99)

Bob Natal (22) walks off the field for the final time in Harrisburg as he watches the Albany-Colonie Yankees celebrate the 1991 Eastern League title on City Island

... and Losing

Manager **Dave Trembley** (1987-89) after a fourth straight loss in May 1988:

"This game is not as hard as we're making it look."

Outfielder **Tony Chance** (1988-89) after a sixth straight loss in May 1988:

"When a team gets in a slump like this, everyone has a glove, even the umpires."

Right fielder and Eastern League MVP **Wes Chamberlain** (1989) after falling to Albany-Colonie in the 1989 finals:

"It was sweet to get here, but it's bitter to lose."

Manager **Mike Quade** (1991-92) after the bullpen suffers a meltdown in April 1992:

"Why don't we talk about eight innings of quality baseball? The people who weren't here don't have to know what happened in the ninth."

Manager **Mike Quade** (1991-92) after a fourth loss in five games in June 1992:
"There are a couple of clubs going in the right direction; we're not one of them."

Manager **Dave Jauss** (1994) after closer **Al Reyes** (1994) gives up three runs in the bottom of the ninth in a stunning 5-4 loss at Binghamton in the pivotal Game 3 of the Eastern League finals:
"I hope to hell a garbage can gets kicked over after this."

Outfielder **Tyrone Horne** (1992-95) after the Senators finish with a league-high 88 victories during the regular season in 1994 before losing to Binghamton in the Eastern League finals:
"Hey, they're the champions on paper, but we're the champions in our hearts."

"People have to accept failure. Like life, you experience failure more than success in baseball and you have to be able to handle it. You have to be able to move on fast after failure, because there's a lot of failure in baseball."
                                                    Manager **Keith Bodie** (2005)

Manager **John Stearns** (2006, 2008-09) during the Senators' franchise-record, 12-game losing streak in April 2009:
"If you're getting your brains beaten in, get mad. Don't hang your head."

Manager **John Stearns** after the Senators' 6-24 start in 2009:
"Even when you play bad, you're supposed to win 40 percent of the time, not 10 percent or whatever it is we've been doing."

"You can save yourself a lot of heartaches if you accept that there are lessons in both winning and losing. And you have to be able to laugh at yourself, because you know world peace doesn't hinge on what we do."
                                                    Manager **Keith Bodie** (2005)

Work Ethic

"If you want something bad enough, work hard enough and long enough it will happen for you."

Manager **Dave Trembley** (1987-89)

Second baseman **Kevin Burdick** (1988-89) after taking part in the Eastern League's Diamond Diplomacy tour of the Soviet Union after the 1989 season:

"I'm amazed at how hard they work. I realize how I've just taken the game for granted, how easy we have it in the States. These kids throw all day and come back and throw more the next. The hitters have blisters on their hands and they still want to hit."

First baseman-outfielder and Eastern League MVP **Cliff Floyd** (1993) on the talent-rich Senators of 1993:

"In this clubhouse, being a first-rounder doesn't mean anything. I still have to work like everybody else."

"If you're going to be on the bench, you have to be prepared. If it's a clutch situation, you have to be doubly prepared. It's your one chance every night."

Outfielder **Jesus Campos** (1996-98)

"A lot of times I'll be taking ground balls out there and getting tired, and then I say to myself, 'Hey, Pete Rose did this, too, so keep going. Just keep going.'"

Shortstop **Josh Labandeira** (2003-05)

Outfielder **Dee Haynes** (2005) on focusing on the game while sitting on the bench:

"Always be on yellow, never red. Always be ready."

"I always play with a chip on my shoulder. I play like that all the time because you don't want to take anything for granted. Nothing is given to you."

Outfielder
Brandon Watson
(2002-03, 2005)

"I come to the park every day like I'm going to play, like I'm catching and hitting fifth. I'm doing the same pregame routine every time. On days when I'm not playing I try to get in a little extra work. You can do all that but there's no substitute for getting up there in a game and seeing pitches. You can't simulate that."

Backup catcher **Jason Brown** (2002-04)

"You have to play with some kind of chip on your shoulder knowing that every day somebody's playing for your job."

Infielder **Dan DeMent** (2005-07)

"I believe in playing the game hard every day. If you can't run out a ball, then we're going to have some issues."

Manager **Tony Beasley** (2011)

"Talk is cheap. I tell players that I don't listen with my ears; I listen with my eyes. You can tell me anything you want, you can say anything you want, but it really has no significance as far as I'm concerned. Actions speak. Words are just time fillers and rhetoric."

Manager **Keith Bodie** (2005)

"The toughest thing you learn as a young manager is knowing you have a problem when winning becomes more important to you than it does to the players."

Manager **Keith Bodie** (2005)

Manager **Tony Beasley** (2011) on pitcher **Oliver Perez** (2011) after the longtime major leaguer joins his Class AA team while still collecting a $12 million salary from the New York Mets, who had released Perez in spring training:

"Put the average Joe down here (in the minors) making $12 million and watch how much of a pain in the butt he'd be. He has been nothing but professional. He respects the coaches. He doesn't buck anything. He goes with the system. He works harder than everybody. He's out early running like a madman. He wants to win. You would never know how many years he's pitched at the major league level."

Work Hazards

Montreal Expos catcher Brian Schneider (1999) on the infamous rat infestation at Philadelphia's now-demolished Veterans Stadium:

"They're not rumors; they're here," he said. "I've seen them in the bullpen here. They're good-size ones, too. They're definitely getting a couple of meals a day."

Just how big? Schneider looked across the clubhouse at the Vet and toward 5-foot-9, 170-pound teammate Jamey Carroll (1998-2000, 2002):

"The rats here," Schneider said with a smile, "are much bigger than Jamey."

Famous Last Words

Montreal Expos player development director **Bill Geivett** in 1995 on former Senators manager and schmooze master **Jim Tracy** (1993):
"He talks and talks on the phone. He talks about fishing, and I don't even fish. When he's telling me about the best baits, I'm doing my paperwork."

Managing partner **Steven Resnick** on Oct. 5, 1994 – six months before signing a 10-year lease with officials from Springfield, Mass., to move the Senators there after the 1996 season:
"People say nothing is forever. That's true. If you asked Baltimore fans if they thought the Colts would move, they would not have believed it. … To say we're going to move would be inappropriate. We have no plans to move."

Pitcher **Joey Eischen** (1993) in September 2004 on the chances of the Expos returning to Montreal in 2005 rather than relocating to Washington, which of course they did a couple of months later:
"I'm not a betting man, but I'll bet a paycheck that we will be back – and I'm not getting a minor league paycheck anymore."

"The Expos know what they got with me. They know how I am. They're not worried about my attitude, because it's not a problem. Before, when I felt something, I had a reaction and I didn't care what the consequences were. Whereas now I know what the consequences are and I don't want to be held back any longer. I let everything now roll off my back. Off the field, I'm a model citizen. I don't get into problems with anybody. Everything (controversial) is just baseball-related. It's just my intensity of working hard and hating to lose."
Milton Bradley (1999) in the spring of 2001, 18 months after his grand slam gives the Senators a fourth straight EL title and four months before Montreal trades him because of his, ahem, attitude

Milton Bradley, author of the pennant-winning grand slam in 1999, returns to City Island as a conquering hero at the Senators' FanFest 2000

A Day in the Life

J ust in case you wanted to know what happened when, to whom and how, here is a day-by-day calendar of all things Harrisburg baseball since the middle of the 19th century. Check out your birthday or anniversary; who knows what may have happened then? For those wanting to look ahead, some of the really cool stuff – you know, minutia – may be found on Jan. 9, Jan. 18, Feb. 12, Feb. 21, Feb. 26, March 2, March 29, April 1, April 13, April 18, April 28, May 2, May 16, May 26, May 30, June 4, June 11, June 19, June 21, July 4, July 9, July 14, July 27, Aug. 1, Aug. 6, Aug. 21, Aug. 31, Sept. 1, Sept. 3, Sept. 6, Sept. 11, Sept. 20, Oct. 4, Oct. 25, Nov. 9, Dec. 9, Dec. 13 and Dec. 20. Come to think of it … interest is in the eyes and mind of the beholder, so you choose for yourself.

January 1
1921: Pitcher **Royce Lint** (1941-42) born in Birmingham, Ala.

Eleanor Engle in 1952

January 2
1926: Infielder **Eleanor Engle**, who in 1952 with the Senators becomes the first woman to sign a pro contract, born in Delmonton, N.J.

January 3
1973: Outfielder **DaRond Stovall** (1996-97) born in St. Louis, Mo.

January 4
1956: Harrisburg Giants infielder **John Beckwith** (1926-27) dies in New York City at age 55.

January 5
1956: Pitching coach **Spin Williams** (1987-88, 1990) born in Davenport, Iowa.

1979: Infielder **Wes Carroll** (2003-04) born in Evansville, Ind.

2005: Free-agent outfielder **Moises Alou** (1989-90) signs a one-year, $7.25 million contract with San Francisco, where he is reunited with his father, Giants manager Felipe Alou. The well-traveled Alou stays with the Giants in 2006 for $5.8 million.

January 6

2000: The Montreal Expos name **Jerry Reuss** (2000) as the Senators' pitching coach.

January 7

2004: Commerce Bank purchases the naming rights to RiverSide Stadium for $3.5 million over 15 years.

January 8

1891: Outfielder **Bud Weiser** (1925) born in Shamokin, Pa.
1921: First baseman **Herb Conyers** (1946-47) born in Cowgill, Mo.

January 9

1979: Outfielder **Hinkey Haines** (1933) dies in Sharon Hills, Pa., at age 80.

1995: University of Massachusetts political science professor **Jerry Mileur**, the Senators' owner since their return to City Island in 1987, finalizes the paperwork to sell his franchise to four investors from suburban Philadelphia for $4.1 million – a nice return on the $85,000 Mileur spends to purchase the team in 1981.

2010: Right fielder **Vladimir Guerrero** (1996) signs a one-year, $5.5 million contract with the Texas Rangers.

JERRY MILEUR

January 10

1898: Harrisburg Giants outfielder **Fats Jenkins** (1924-27) born in New York City.
1900: Harrisburg Giants infielder **John Beckwith** (1926-27) born in Louisville, Ky.
1996: Boston trades pitcher **Shayne Bennett** (1996-97) to Montreal in a five-player deal that sends future, albeit briefly, Senators infielder **Wil Cordero** (2005) to the Red Sox.

JOSH JOHNSON

January 11

1974: Pitcher **Jake Chapman** (2000-01) born in Lafayette, Ind.

1986: Shortstop **Josh Johnson** (2010-13) born in Tampa, Fla.

2006: The Nationals name four-time All-Star catcher **John Stearns** (2006, 2008-09) as the Senators' manager, replacing **Keith Bodie** (2005).

January 12

1968: Hitting coach **Steve Phillips** (1999) born in Hamilton, Ohio.

January 13
1987: Rick Redd (1987-91) becomes the first general manager in the Senators' modern era.

January 14
1962: Manager **Les Mann** (1934) dies in Pasadena, Calif., at age 69.

1986: After Cleveland selects pitcher Jeff Shaw with the first pick of the January amateur draft, Pittsburgh picks future All-Star outfielder **Moises Alou** (1989-90).

2004: Right fielder **Vladimir Guerrero** (1996) signs as a free agent with the Angels, for whom he will play six seasons and be named the American League MVP in 2004.

January 15
1965: Catcher **Jeff Banister** (1988-90) born in Weatherford, Okla.

1982: Infielder-coach **Melvin Dorta** (2004-07, 2013) born in Valencia, Venz.

1982: Pitcher **Armando Galarraga** (2005) born in Cumana, Venz.

2006: Team Canada selects utility player **Matt Stairs** (1991) for the inaugural World Baseball Classic.

January 16
1957: Manager **Dave Jauss** (1994) born in Chicago.

January 17
2013: Team Canada picks pitcher **Shawn Hill** (2003-04, 2006) and first baseman-outfielder **Jimmy Van Ostrand** (2012-13) for the third World Baseball Classic.

1966: Pitcher **Carl Keliipuleole** (1991) born in Guam.

1975: First baseman **Brad Fullmer** (1996-97) born in Chatsworth, Calif.

BRAD FULLMER

1977: Hitting coach **Troy Gingrich** (2008-11) born in West Corvina, Calif.

2005: Nationals name **Keith Bodie** (2005) as the Senators' manager.

January 18
1963: Pitcher **Bill Sampen** (1988-89) born in Lincoln, Ill.

1991: The Senators sign a four-year contract to become Montreal's Class AA affiliate, beginning a relationship that lasts well beyond the Expos' exodus from Montreal to Washington, D.C. in 2005.

January 19
1963: Outfielder and manager **Scott Little** (1988, 2007) born in East St. Louis, Ill.

1975: First baseman **Fernando Seguignol** (1998) born in Bocas del Toro, Panama.

January 20

1965: Future pitching coach **Tommy John** (2002) is part of a three-team, eight-player, flowchart of a trade that sends him, along with outfielder Tommie Agee and catcher Johnny Romano from the Indians to the White Sox with catcher Cam Carreon going from Chicago to Cleveland; and the White Sox dealing pitcher Fred Talbot, and outfielders Jim Landis and Mike Hershberger to the Kansas City Athletics, who then send outfielder Rocky Colavito – the headliner in the deal – to the Indians.

January 21

2004: Outfielder **Johnny Blatnik** (1946) dies in Lansing, Ohio, at age 82.

January 22

2004: Pitching coach **Tommy John** (2002) leaves the Expos' organization to become the manager of the Yankees' short-season Class A team on Staten Island.

2012: Longtime Philadelphia Phillies broadcaster **Andy Musser**, a batboy on City Island in the early 1950s, dies in Wynnewood, Pa., at age 74.

January 23

1923: Pitcher-outfielder **Cot Deal** (1942) born in Arapaho, Okla.

1962: Pitching coach **Tom Signore** (2001) born in North Haven, Conn.

1983: Pitcher **Cookie Cuccurullo** (1942) dies in West Orange, N.J., at age 64.

January 24

1953: Harrisburg Giants Hall of Fame first baseman **Ben Taylor** (1925) dies in Baltimore at age 64.

1980: Player-manager **Buck Etchison** (1952) dies in Cambridge, Md., at age 64.

RICK SWEET

January 25

1966: Pitcher **Richie Lewis** (1991) born in Muncie, Ind.

1968: Infielder **Chris Martin** (1991-93) born in Los Angeles.

1978: San Diego trades future Senators pitching coach **Dave Tomlin** (1994) to Cleveland for Hall of Fame pitcher Gaylord Perry. Perry promptly wins 21 games for the Padres and the 1978 National League Cy Young Award with future Senators manager **Rick Sweet** (1998-99) serving as his personal catcher.

January 26

1979: Outfielder **Kenny Kelly** (2005) born in Plant City, Fla.

January 27

1915: Player-manager **Buck Etchison** (1952) born in Baltimore.

1970: Right fielder **Kevin Northrup** (1994-95) born in Kingston, N.Y.

1972: Second baseman **Mike Hardge** (1993-94) born in Fort Hood, Tex.

2003: Manager **Dave Trembley** (1987-89) returns to the Eastern League as the manager for Baltimore's affiliate in Bowie, Md.

January 28

1972: Pitcher **Steve Falteisek** (1995-96) born in Mineola, N.Y.

1978: Shortstop **Tomas de la Rosa** (1999) born in Santo Domingo, D.R.

January 29

1969: The Washington Senators fire **Jim Lemon** (1949) after one season and a 65-96 record as their manager.

TYLER MOORE

1996: Less than two years after buying him from Montreal for $100,000, the Red Sox trade outfielder **Glenn Murray** (1993) to Philadelphia in a six-player trade that sends pitcher Heathcliff Slocumb to Boston.

January 30

1925: Pitcher **Brooks Lawrence** (1951), the Senators' first black pitcher, born in Springfield, Ohio.

1954: Pitching coach **Joe Kerrigan** (1991) born in Philadelphia.

1973: Catcher **Bob Henley** (1996-97) born in Mobile, Ala.

1987: First baseman **Tyler Moore** (2011) born in Brandon, Miss.

January 31

1971: Manager **Steve Yerkes** (1924) dies in Lansdale, Pa., at age 82.

February 1

1890: Player-manager **Earle Mack** (1917), the son of Philadelphia A's Hall of Fame manager Connie Mack, born in Spencer, Mass.

1928: Catcher-infielder **Hughie Jennings** (1890) dies in Scranton, Pa., at age 58.

2010: Shortstop **Orlando Cabrera** (1997) signs a one-year contract with Cincinnati for $2.02 million.

February 2

1988: Pitcher **Brad Peacock** (2010-11) born in Palm Beach, Fla.

February 3
2010: Brewers claim pitcher **Marco Estrada** (2008) off waivers from the Nationals.

February 4
1888: Player-manager **Rankin Johnson** (1925-26) born in Burnet, Tex.
1967: Player-manager **Earle Mack** (1917) dies in Upper Darby, Pa., at age 77.

February 5
1979: Outfielder **Brett Roneberg** (2002) born in Melbourne, Australia.

February 6
2004: The Expos name former major leaguers **Rob Ducey** and **Mark Grater** as the Senators' hitting and pitching coaches for the 2004 season.
2004: Catcher **Tom Prince** (1987) formerly retires to become manager of Pittsburgh's short-season, Class A team in Williamsport.

February 7
1964: Infielder **Bien Figueroa** (1994) born in Santo Domingo, D.R.

February 8
1918: Pitcher **Cookie Cuccurullo** (1942) born in Asbury Park, N.J.

February 9
1975: Right fielder **Vladimir Guerrero** (1996) born in Nizao, D.R.
1976: A special Negro Leagues committee elects Harrisburg Giants player-manager **Oscar Charleston** (1924-27) to the Hall of Fame.

CHIEF MEYERS

February 10
1916: Catcher **Chief Meyers** (1906) is waived by the New York Giants and claimed by with the Brooklyn Dodgers and Boston Braves; a coin flip sends him to Brooklyn.

February 11
1956: Pitcher **Joseph Myers** (1908-12) dies in Delaware City, Del., at age 73.

2001: A little more than four months after third baseman **John Wehner** (1990) hits the final homer there, Pittsburgh's Three Rivers Stadium is imploded to create parking spaces for the new PNC Park.

February 12
1965: Pitcher **Stan Fansler** (1988) born in Elkins, W.Va.

2002: Fretting over the prospect of losing their jobs with Major League Baseball threatening to fold the foundering Expos, the Senators lose their previously announced 2002 coaching staff as manager **Eric Fox**, pitching coach **Tom Signore** and hitting coach **Matt Raleigh** accept offers – along with $5,000 bonuses for jumping organizations – to join former Montreal owner Jeff Loria with the Florida Marlins. **Dave Huppert**, **Tommy John** and **Frank Cacciatore** will replace Fox, Signore and Raleigh as Harrisburg's staff.

February 13
1956: Manager **Keith Bodie** (2005) born in Brooklyn, N.Y.

1969: Pitcher **Michael Mimbs** (1994) born in Macon, Ga.

1987: Pitcher **Ryan Perry** (2012-13) born in Pomona, Calif.

February 14
1931: Outfielder **Joe Caffie** (1951), the Senators' first black position player, born in Ramer, Ala.

1989: Catcher **Derek Norris** (2011) born in Goddard, Kan.

February 15
1866: Player-manager and Hall of Famer **Billy Hamilton** (1905-06) born in Newark, N.J.

1974: Pitcher **Ugueth Urbina** (1993-94) born in Caracas, Venz.

JOE CAFFIE

February 16
1915: Rather than give him a pay raise, Philadelphia A's manager Connie Mack releases Hall of Fame pitcher **Chief Bender** (1902).

1964: Shortstop **Rico Rossy** (1989) born in San Juan, P.R.

1974: Shortstop **Luis Figueroa** (2002) born in Bayamon, P.R.

1987: Pitcher **Tommy Milone** (2010) born in Saugus, Calif.

2011: Shortstop **Orlando Cabrera** (1997) signs a one-year, $1 million contract with Cleveland for 2011 – his 15th and final season in the majors.

February 17

1893: Manager **Eddie Onslow** (1931-33) born in Meadville, Pa.

1956: Outfielder **Kip Selbach** (1907-08, 1910) dies in Columbus, Ohio, at age 83.

February 18

1922: Catcher **Joe Tipton** (1946), whom Connie Mack acquires for the A's in 1949 for Hall of Fame second baseman Nellie Fox, born in McCaysville, Ga.

1974: Infielder **Jamey Carroll** (1998-2000, 2002) born in Evansville, Ind.

2011: Vladimir Guerrero (1996), now a fulltime designated hitter, signs a one-year, $7.6 million contract with Baltimore for his 16th and final season in the majors.

February 19

1965: Pitching coach **Wayne Rosenthal** (1999) born in Brooklyn, N.Y.

1971: Pitcher **Miguel Batista** (1993-94) born in Santo Domingo, D.R.

February 20

1947: Major league pitcher **Tom Buskey** born in Harrisburg, Pa.

February 21

2011: Outfielder **Bryce Harper** (2011, 2013), the top pick of the 2010 amateur draft, has yet to play an inning as a pro but finds himself inundated by autograph hounds after his first spring training workout with the Nationals in Viera, Fla.

RONDELL WHITE

February 22

2013: Pitcher **Stephen Strasburg** (2010-11) is rusty in his first start for the Nationals since being shut down in early September 2012. Strasburg, whose 2012 season is cut short as a precaution following reconstructive arm surgery in 2010, begins the bottom of the first inning of his spring training debut by allowing a single to Kirk Nieuwenhuis and a wind-aided homer by Ruben Tejada in a game won by the Mets 5-3 in the Port St. Lucie, Fla.

February 23

1972: Center fielder **Rondell White** (1992-93, 1996) born in Milledgeville, Ga.

February 24

1991: Outfielder **Joe Munson** (1925), the Eastern League's first Triple Crown winner in 1925 and its last .400 hitter, dies in Drexel Hill, Pa., at age 91.

February 25

1979: Shortstop **Josh Labandeira** (2003-05) born in Tulare, Calif.

February 26

1987: Harrisburg mayor **Stephen Reed** announces the Senators' new ballpark on City Island will be called RiverSide Stadium. Reed also names the playing surface "All-America Field," but that name is quickly forgotten.

2012: Third baseman **Ryan Zimmerman** (2005) agrees to a $100 million contract extension to remain with the Nationals through the 2019 season.

February 27

1968: Infielder **Matt Stairs** (1991) born in St. John, New Brunswick, Canada.

February 28

2012: Outfielder **Bryce Harper** (2011, 2013) strikes out twice in his spring training debut with the Nationals, but that hardly is a harbinger of things to come as the 19-year-old Harper is named the National League Rookie of the Year after helping Washington win the N.L. East title.

February 29

1996: Work continues on City Island in the aftermath of January flooding that fills both clubhouses with water and mud after two of six watertight doors designed to protect the clubhouses are inadvertently left open. The stadium needs $5 million in repairs before reopening in April.

March 1

1944: The Washington Senators trade outfielder **Gene Moore** (1932), the first Harrisburg player to be selected for a major league All-Star Game, to the St. Louis Browns for Hall of Fame catcher Rick Farrell.

1994: Catcher **Joe Tipton** (1946) dies in Birmingham, Ala., at age 72.

March 2

1985: Pitcher **Zech Zinicola** (2006-12) born in Loma Linda, Calif.

2005: Pitcher **Tony Armas Jr.** (1999) starts and works two shutout innings of the Nationals' first-ever exhibition game against the New York Mets in Viera, Fla. The game, a 5-3 Washington victory, is the team's first since relocating after 35 seasons in Montreal.

2012: The College Baseball Hall of Fame names outfielder **Brad Wilkerson** (1999-2000) to its seventh annual class of inductees that includes Hall of Famer Lou Brock and two-time American League batting champion Nomar Garciaparra.

March 3

1964: Catcher and future Nationals coach **Trent Jewett** (1990) born in Dallas, Tex.

March 4

1974: Pitcher **Tommy Phelps** (1996-99) born in Seoul, South Korea.
1976: Infielder **Hiram Bocachica** (1997-98) born in Ponce, P.R.

March 5

1971: Outfielder **Jeffrey Hammonds** (2005) born in Plainfield, N.J.

March 6

HARRY O'NEILL

1902: Harrisburg Giants infielder **Rev Cannady** (1925-27) born in Norfolk, Va.
1945: Catcher **Harry O'Neill** (1940) is killed during the Battle of Iwo Jima, becoming the second of two former major leaguers – Washington Senators outfielder Elmer Gedeon being the other – to die in World War II. O'Neill was 27.
1976: Catcher **Scott Sandusky** (2000-03) born in Denver, Colo.
1986: Pitcher **Ross Detwiler** (2009-10) born in St. Louis, Mo.
2002: The Expos name onetime Orioles catcher **Dave Huppert** and longtime major leaguer **Tommy John** as the Senators' manager and pitching coach for the 2002 season.

March 7

1968: Pitcher **Denis Boucher** (1996) born in Montreal.
1977: Shortstop **Josh Reding** (2000-02) born in Bellflower, Calif.

March 8

1912: Catcher **Ray Mueller** (1932-34) born in Pittsburg, Kan.

March 9

1986: Pitcher **Craig Stammen** (2008) born in Versailles, Ohio.
1994: First baseman **Elbie Fletcher** (1934) dies in Milton, Mass., at age 77.

March 10

1921: Outfielder **Johnny Blatnik** (1946) born in Bridgeport, Ohio.
2006: Shairon Martis (2006, 2008, 2011) throws the first no-hitter in the World Baseball Classic to lead the Netherlands over Panama 10-0 in Puerto Rico.

March 11
1899: Onetime catcher and infielder **Hughie Jennings** (1890), the first Harrisburg player elected to the Hall of Fame, is traded from Baltimore to Brooklyn.
1971: Pitcher **Rodney Henderson** (1993-95) born in Greensburg, Ky.

March 12
1957: Manager **Mike Quade** (1991-92) born in Evanston, Ill.
1976: Pitcher **Bryan Hebson** (2000-02) born in Columbus, Ga.
1978: Outfielder **Gene Moore** (1932) dies in Jackson, Miss., at age 68.

March 13
1989: Catcher **Sandy Leon** (2012-13) born in Maracaibo, Venz.

March 14
1969: Outfielder **Jalal Leach** (1996) born in San Francisco.

March 15
1980: Infielder **Freddie Bynum** (2009) born in Wilson, N.C.

SANDY LEON

March 16
2000: In a three-team trade involving all first basemen, the Expos deal **Brad Fullmer** (1996-97) to Toronto with the Blue Jays shipping David Segui to Texas and the Rangers sending Lee Stevens to Montreal, which in two years flips Stevens to Cleveland in a flop of a deal that costs the Expos top prospects and future All-Stars in shortstop **Brandon Phillips** (2001-02), pitcher **Cliff Lee** (2002) and center fielder Grady Sizemore.

March 17
1968: First baseman **Dan Masteller** (1996) born in Toledo, Ohio.
1993: Pitcher **Lefty Hefflefinger** (1929, 1931-35) dies in Harrisburg, Pa., at age 80.

March 18
1882: Pitcher **Joseph Myers** (1908-12) born in Wilmington, Del.
1916: First baseman **Elbie Fletcher** (1934) born in Milton, Mass.
1977: First baseman-outfielder **Terrmel Sledge** (2001-02) born in Fayetteville, N.C.
2012: The Nationals assign outfielder **Bryce Harper** (2011, 2013) to Class AAA Syracuse so he may further develop his skills in center field before an inevitable promotion to the majors.

March 19

1968: Pitcher **Pete Young** (1991) born in Meadville, Miss.

1973: Pitcher **Scott Mitchell** (1997-99, 2001) born in San Pablo, Calif.

1984: Pitcher **Erik Arnesen** (2009-11) born in Princeton, N.J.

March 20

1966: Pitcher **Blas Minor** (1990) born in Merced, Calif.

1987: Pitcher **Brett Gideon** (1987-88) is the starter in the modern-era Senators' first-ever exhibition game, a 5-4 victory over the Birmingham Barons in Bradenton, Fla.

BRETT GIDEON

March 21

1970: Pitcher **Rick DeHart** (1993, 1995-96) born in Topeka, Kan.

1974: Pitcher **Rodney Stevenson** (1997-2000) born in Columbus, Ga.

March 22

1882: Outfielder **Jimmy Sebring** (1908) born in Liberty, Pa.

March 23

1928: Outfielder **Jim Lemon** (1949) born in Covington, Va.

1994: The Expos sell outfielder **Glenn Murray** (1993), whose 26 homers in 1993 tie him with **Cliff Floyd** (1993) for the most in modern franchise history, to Boston for $100,000.

March 24

1872: Outfielder **Kip Selbach** (1907-08, 1910) born in Columbus, Ohio.

1961: First baseman **Al Chambers**, the top pick of the 1979 amateur draft out of Harrisburg High, born in Harrisburg, Pa.

March 25

1969: Pitching coach **Paul Menhart** (2012-13) born in St. Louis, Mo.

1985: Pitcher **Hassan Pena** (2010-11) born in Havana, Cuba.

1989: Pittsburgh trades shortstop **Felix Fermin** (1987) to Cleveland for shortstop Jay Bell.

March 26

1997: The Expos trade first baseman-outfielder **Cliff Floyd** (1993) to the Florida Marlins for pitcher Dustin Hermanson and outfielder Joe Orsulak.

March 27

1970: Pitcher **Derek Aucoin** (1994-95) born in Lachine, Quebec.
1978: Outfielder **Dermal Brown** (2005) born in Bronx, N.Y.

March 28

1953: Outfielder **Jim Thorpe** (1915) dies in Lomita, Calif., at age 65.

March 29

1910: Pitcher **Bill "Bullfrog" Dietrich** (1931) born in Philadelphia.
2000: Third baseman **Shane Andrews** (1993) becomes the first player to homer in an Opening Day game played outside the United States as the Cubs beat the Mets 5-3 in Tokyo. Andrews' two-run homer comes in the seventh inning off Dennis Cook and gives Chicago a 4-1 lead.

SHANE ANDREWS

March 30

1978: Shortstop **Billy Cox** (1940-41) dies in Harrisburg, Pa., at age 68.
1987: Pitcher **Shairon Martis** (2006, 2008, 2011) born in Willemstad, Curacao.
2008: Third baseman **Ryan Zimmerman** (2005) hits a two-out, ninth-inning solo homer off Atlanta's Peter Moylan to give Washington a 3-2 victory in the first game played at Nationals Park.

March 31

1980: Pitcher **Chien-Ming Wang** (2011-12) born in Tainan City, Taiwan.

April 1

1987: The Senators need only eight hours to sell out April 11's Opening Day, Harrisburg's first opener since 1952. David Ellis, a carpenter from Harrisburg, is the first in line for tickets.
1996: Plate umpire John McSherry suffers a fatal heart attack as Montreal's **Rondell White** (1992-93, 1996) prepares for a 1-1pitch from Pete Schourek in the top of the first inning of the Expos' season opener in Cincinnati. McSherry is only 51 years old, but grossly overweight at 380-plus pounds.

David Ellis, right, in 1987 with Senators GM Rick Redd

150

April 2

1869: Hall of Famer **Hughie Jennings** (1890) born in Pittston, Pa.

April 3

1968: Shortstop **Mike Lansing** (1992) born in Rawlins, Wyo.

1975: Pitcher **Sugar Cain** (1931) dies in Atlanta, Ga., at age 67.

1990: Outfielder **Destin Hood** (2012-13) born in Mobile, Ala.

2000: Outfielder **Vladimir Guerrero** (1996) homers twice in the Expos' 10-4 loss to the Dodgers, joining Gabe Kapler, **Ivan Rodriguez** (2011), Jason Giambi, Tony Batista and Shannon Stewart in making history as one of a record six players with multi-homer games on Opening Day.

2006: Pitcher **Royce Lint** (1941-42) dies in Portland, Ore., at age 85.

MIKE LANSING

April 4

1999: With **Mike Lansing** (1992) playing at second base and going 2-for-5 with two singles, Colorado beats San Diego 8-2 in the majors' first season opener played in Mexico.

2005: Outfielders **Brad Wilkerson** (1999-2000) and **Terrmel Sledge** (2001-02) pick up the Nationals' first hit and homer, but they are not enough in an 8-4 loss at Philadelphia.

2010: Outfielder **Dermal Brown** (2005) homers twice to lead the Seibu Lions over the Nippon Ham Fighters in Japan. His second homer also is the 90,000[th] hit in league history.

April 5

1907: Pitcher **Sugar Cain** (1931) born in Macon, Ga.

1971: Outfielder **Mark Charbonnet** (1995) born in Harbor City, Calif.

1976: Pitcher **Matt Blank** (1999) born in Texarkana, Tex.

1996: Ten minutes before the Senators depart for their season opener at Trenton, pitcher **Esteban Yan** is pulled off the team bus and told the Expos have sold him to Baltimore.

2002: Only hours before his scheduled start at Altoona is snowed out, pitcher **Phil Seibel** (2002) is traded by the Expos to the Mets, along with outfielder **Matt Watson** (2002) and pitcher **Scott Strickland** (1999) for shortstop **Luis Figueroa** (2002), and pitchers Bruce Chen, Dicky Gonzalez and **Saul Rivera** (2002, 2004-05). Figueroa and Rivera become mainstays that season on the last Harrisburg team to reach the EL finals until 2013.

2010: Utility player **Matt Stairs** (1991) flies out as a pinch-hitter in the Padres' 6-3 loss at Arizona, marking his appearance with a 12th different franchise and breaking Deacon McGuire's 98-year-old record for most teams by a position player.

2011: Chris Young (2003) becomes the first pitcher in the Mets' 50 seasons to get two hits in one inning with a pair of singles in the third off Cole Hamels during a 7-1 victory at Philadelphia. Young finishes 3-for-3 with his only win in an injury-marred season.

April 6

1909: Utility player **Doggie Miller** (1893) dies in Ridgewood, N.Y., at age 44.

2005: Outfielder **Brad Wilkerson** (1999-2000) hits for the Nationals' first cycle in a 7-3 victory at Philadelphia, becoming only the 20th player in history to twice hit for the cycle in a career.

2006: Outfielder **Moises Alou** (1989-90) is one of three sons of former major leaguers to score – Barry Bonds and Lance Niekro being the others – on Pedro Feliz's bases-loaded double in the third inning of the Giants' 6-4 victory over Atlanta in San Francisco.

2009: Outfielder-designated hitter **Vladimir Guerrero** (1996) drives in a run for the Angels in a 3-0 victory over Oakland, giving him 19 RBIs on Opening Day and breaking the major league record he had shared with Hall of Famer Frank Robinson and Jeff Kent.

BRAD WILKERSON

April 7

1964: Pitcher **Johnny Tillman** (1928-30), who in 1928 serves up Babe Ruth's tape-measure homer in an exhibition game on City Island, dies in Harrisburg, Pa., at age 70.

2008: An intimate but chilled gathering of only 601 watches the Senators beat Erie 12-5 – the smallest crowd to see a game on City Island since baseball returned there in 1987.

April 8

2003: Pitchers Fernando Cabrera, Aaron Myette and Jose Vargas combine to no-hit the Senators 15-0 at Akron's Canal Park. The game easily is the poorest played by the modern-era Senators, who allow 15 runs on 18 hits while walking eight and committing six errors.

2006: The Senators beat Erie 3-1 on City Island, marking the first time in their modern era that they start a season 3-0. Alas, the first loss comes 24 hours later.

April 9

1975: First baseman **Talmadge Nunnari** (1999-2001, 2003) born in Pensacola, Fla.

1993: Shortstop **Edgar Tovar** (1993, 1995) drives home the winning run with a ninth-inning single as the Senators beat

EDGAR TOVAR

Albany-Colonie 3-2 on City Island for the first of their 100 victories en route to winning the Eastern League title.

1994: The Trenton Thunder, formerly the London Tigers, pick up their first-ever victory, beating the Senators 4-0 on City Island.

April 10

1971: Pitcher **Al Reyes** (1994) born in San Cristobal, D.R.

1972: Pitcher **Shayne Bennett** (1996-97) born in Adelaide, South Australia.

1997: The Senators turn out to be honored guests in the first game at Akron's new Canal Park, helping open the $30 million ballpark with a 13-2 loss to the Aeros.

2010: The first game at newly renovated, $45.1 million Metro Bank Park is a high school contest between Greenwood and Newport with Greenwood winning 5-3.

April 11

1875: Manager **Win Clark** (1927) born in Circleville, Ohio.

1987: RiverSide Stadium opens with a crowd of 4,083 watching the Senators play the first game of their modern era, an 11-5 loss to Vermont. Vermont's Chris Jones hits the first home run in the new $1.4 million stadium; **Crash Brown** (1987) later hits the Senators' first homer.

1991: Catcher **Bob Natal** (1991) hits three homers and drives in eight during a 21-5 rout of London on City Island.

2000: Kirk Rueter (1993) throws the first pitch for the Giants at newly minted Pac Bell Park in San Francisco but is the losing pitcher as the Dodgers win 6-5.

2003: Second baseman **Jose Vidro** (1995-96, 2006) goes 3-for-4 with three RBIs in Montreal's 10-0 rout of the Mets in the first of the Expos' 22 home-away-from-home games at Puerto Rico's Hiram Bithorn Stadium.

CRASH BROWN

2004: The Senators win 4-2 at Bowie for their 1,000th victory as Montreal's AA affiliate.

2010: Pitcher **Stephen Strasburg** (2010-11), the top pick of the 2009 draft, makes his pro debut, going five innings and earning the victory as the Senators win 6-4 at Altoona.

April 12

1876: Pitcher and future Hall of Famer **Vic Willis** (1895) born in Cecil County, Md.

1936: Infielder **George Fiall** (Giants 1924-25, 1927) dies in New York City at age 35.

2007: After six losses to open the season – matching the 1999 team's record for the worst start in modern franchise history – the Senators beat Erie 6-2 on City Island.

April 13

1966: Right fielder **Wes Chamberlain** (1989) born in Chicago.

1996: Infielder **Carlos Garcia** (1989-90) hits the 8,000th homer in Pirates' history during the fourth inning of a 9-3 victory over the Expos at Pittsburgh's Three Rivers Stadium.

1999: After a bench-clearing brawl against Altoona on City Island, the focal point of the melee – Senators center fielder **Milton Bradley** (1999) – is ejected from the game and then spits gum at umpire Tim Pasch. Bradley receives a five-game suspension and a $500 fine from the Eastern League, as well as a two-game suspension from the Expos.

April 14

1971: Pitcher **Carlos Perez** (1994) born in San Cristobal, D.R.

1982: First baseman **Josh Whitesell** (2006-07) born in Durham, N.C.

2005: Catcher **Brian Schneider** (1999) is on the receiving end of the ceremonial first pitch by President George W. Bush before the erstwhile Expos play their first game as the new Washington Nationals at RFK Stadium. The Nationals win the game 5-3, beating Arizona and former Senators pitcher **Javier Vazquez** (1997).

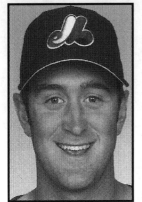

BRIAN SCHNEIDER

April 15

1959: Manager **Win Clark** (1927) dies in Los Angeles at age 84.

1968: Pitcher **Billy Brewer** (1992) born in Fort Worth, Tex.

1978: Center fielder **Milton Bradley** (1999) born in Harbor City, Calif.

2010: With the $45.1 million stadium overhaul complete, the Senators use three singles and two walks to cobble together two runs in the bottom of the ninth and beat New Britain 6-5 before a home opener crowd of 6,361.

April 16

1867: Outfielder **Piggy Ward** (1893) born in Chambersburg, Pa.

1979: Pitcher **Justin Wayne** (2001-02) born in Honolulu.

2000: The Senators lose to Akron 8-3 on City Island, falling to 1-8 for the worst start in the team's modern era. They recover to reach the EL playoffs for a fifth straight season.

2009: Pitcher **Cliff Lee** (2002) scatters seven hits and one run over six innings to lead Cleveland over New York 10-2 in the first game at new Yankee Stadium.

2010: Pitcher **Stephen Strasburg** (2010-11) makes his much-anticipated City Island debut. Strasburg draws a then-record crowd of 7,895 before waiting out a couple of hours of delays for rain, lightning and a power failure that limit him to less than three innings of work against New Britain.

April 17

1957: Manager **Dave Huppert** (2002) born in South Gate, Calif.

1994: Despite having three relievers listed on his lineup card, Portland manager Carlos Tosca uses former Senators infielder **Chris Malinoski** (1992) to pitch the 12th inning of a 4-4 game on City Island. The game ends quickly as **Mark Grudzielanek** (1994) singles to left on Malinoski's 1-0 pitch and scores when **Tyrone Horne** (1992-95) lines Malinoski's 1-1 changeup to left-center for a double.

2008: Center fielder **Roger Bernadina** (2007-08) hits a grand slam in an 8-4 victory over New Hampshire, his third in two seasons to become the first Senator to hit three career slams since the team rejoins the Eastern League in 1987.

April 18

1981: Manager **Dave Huppert** (2002), then a Baltimore prospect, is the starting catcher for Class AAA Rochester against Pawtucket in a game that lasts a record 32 innings before being suspended and resumed six weeks later for a 33rd and final inning. Huppert is behind the plate for 31 innings before being lifted for a pinch-hitter in the top of the 32nd.

1999: The Senators finally win a game – actually, two with a doubleheader sweep at Akron – after starting the season 0-6, the longest season-opening skid in modern franchise history.

DAVE HUPPERT

April 19

1920: Washington Senators pitcher **Al Schacht** (1915) beats the Athletics 7-0 for the only shutout of his brief, injury-shortened stay in majors before embarking on a second career as the "Clown Prince of Baseball."

1994: After struggling to hit left-handed, second baseman **Mike Hardge** (1993-94) junks the Expos' in-season experiment to turn him into a switch-hitter and decides to bat right-handed in the 12th inning against Reading. Hardge promptly drills a two-run homer off right-hander Craig Holman for an 8-6, walk-off victory on City Island.

MIKE HARDGE

April 20

1881: Outfielder **Steamer Flanagan** (1913) born in Kingston, Pa.

2013: With **Ryan Zimmerman** (2005) out with a sore hamstring, the Nationals promote third baseman **Anthony Rendon** (2012-13) from City Island to Citi Field in New York, where his major league debut comes the next day against the Mets.

April 21

1947: Outfielder **Steamer Flanagan** (1913) dies in Wilkes-Barre, Pa., at age 66.

April 22

2013: In one of the most dominating performances ever on City Island, Reading's Jesse Biddle strikes out 16 Senators in a game in which he is perfect through six innings. Biddle allows a walk and a single in the seventh, his final inning in Reading's 3-2 victory. Biddle's 16 strikeouts tie the 1994 total by Bowie's Jimmy Haynes for most by an opposing pitcher against the Senators in their modern era. Just for fun, Biddle picks up two doubles, his first extra-base hits as a pro.

April 23

2002: Valentino Pascucci (2001-02), **Matt Cepicky** (2001-02) and **Scott Hodges** (2000-02, 2005) homer on three straight pitches from Geraldo Padua in the eighth inning as the Senators beat Altoona 4-2 on City Island.

April 24

2001: Ron Chiavacci (2001-03) strikes out 10 in a 2-1 win over Altoona on City Island, becoming the first modern-era Senator with at least 10 strikeouts in three straight starts.

April 25

1900: Infielder **George Fiall** (Giants 1924-25, 1927) born in Charleston, S.C.

1987: Infielder **Danny Espinosa** (2010) born in Santa Ana, Calif.

VALENTINO PASCUCCI

April 26

1973: Infielder **Geoff Blum** (1996, 1998) born in Redwood City, Calif.

1976: Pitcher **Scott Strickland** (1999) born in Houston, Tex.

1982: Infielder **Alejandro Machado** (2005) born in Caracas, Venz.

1994: Concerned over his finances, the National Association of Professional Baseball Leagues rejects a bid by **Van Farber** to become the Senators' next owner.

2000: **Troy Mattes** (1999-2000, 2003) comes within two outs of pitching the first no-hitter in the Senators' modern era before Altoona's Alex Hernandez singles with one out in the ninth inning on City Island. The Senators win 3-2 in 10 innings.

TROY MATTES

April 27

2000: Pitcher **Brooks Lawrence** (1951) dies in Springfield, Ohio, at age 75.

2003: Every Senator picks up either a hit, run or RBI during an 11-run third inning in a 12-2 rout of Reading on City Island. The runs are the most scored in one inning at River-Side Stadium since the Senators' return in 1987. The Senators duplicate the feat three weeks later, scoring 11 times in the ninth inning of a 14-3 victory at Erie.

2005: Shortstop **Mark Grudzielanek** (1994) hits for the cycle in his first four at-bats during the Cardinals' 6-3 victory over the Brewers in St. Louis. Grudzielanek grounds out in his final at-bat against former Senator **Tommy Phelps** (1996-99).

April 28

1981: Pitcher **Shawn Hill** (2003-04, 2006) born in Mississauga, Ontario.

1993: Kirk Rueter (1993) throws eight scoreless innings as the Senators beat Canton-Akron 9-1 for their 12th victory in 15 games to move atop the Eastern League standings, where they remain for rest of the season.

2001: A crowd of 6,337 – then the largest ever to attend an April game on City Island – watches the Senators beat Reading 6-1.

2003: Seung Song (2002-03) becomes the first Senator in their modern era to throw a no-hitter as he beats Erie 2-1 on City Island. The no-hitter is not without controversy as an apparently clean bunt single by Nook Logan in the ninth inning is ruled a throwing error on Seung, even though the speedy Logan easily beats Seung's throw to first.

SEUNG SONG

2012: Bryce Harper (2011, 2013) makes his major league debut at Dodger Stadium, starting in left field for the Nationals and going 1-for-3 with a double off Chad Billingsley in the seventh inning and a sacrifice fly off Javy Guerra in the ninth before Washington falls 4-3 in 10 innings.

April 29

1978: Pitcher **Tony Armas Jr.** (1999, 2006) born in Puerto Piritu, Venz.

1993: Catcher **Miah Bradbury** (1993) refuses a promotion to Class AAA Ottawa and retires, leaving coach **Greg Fulton** (1991-93) as the Senators' temporary backup catcher until **Lance Rice** (1993-94) arrives a week later.

1994: Kirk Rueter (1993), then with the Expos, beats the Pirates 3-2 to become the first major leaguer since Fernando Valenzuela in 1981 to begin his career with a 10-0 record.

April 30

1996: Third baseman **Jeff King** (1987-88) becomes only the third major leaguer – Hall of Famers Willie McCovey and Andre Dawson being the first two – to homer twice in one inning for the second time in his career. These two come off John Smiley and Tim Pugh in the top of the fourth inning in the Pirates' 10-7 victory at Cincinnati. Less than nine months earlier, on Aug. 8, 1995, King homers off Sergio Valdez and Terry Mulholland in the top of the second inning of the Pirates' 9-5 victory at San Francisco.

2000: T.J. Tucker (1999-2001) becomes the first pitcher in the Senators' modern era to hit higher than ninth in the batting order as manager **Doug Sisson** (1999-2000) places him seventh, ahead of catcher **Jaime Malave** (1999-2000) and third baseman **Garret Osilka** (2000). Tucker grounds out and pops out in an 8-5 victory over Reading on City Island. The Expos, the Senators' major league affiliate, are not amused by Sisson's tactics and tell the manager to restrain himself from entertaining any such thoughts in the future.

2009: The Senators fall 9-3 in Akron to extend their losing streak to a modern franchise-record 12 games, a skid that ends the next day with a 4-2 victory over Reading on City Island.

May 1

1996: Right fielder **Vladimir Guerrero** (1996) arrives on City Island and promptly hits his first Class AA homer on his way to an MVP season in the Eastern League.

GREG FULTON

May 2

1993: Three days after backup catcher **Miah Bradbury** (1993) abruptly retires, coach-turned-player **Greg Fulton** (1991-93) reluctantly finds himself behind the plate when **Rob Fitzpatrick** (1993-95) is ejected in the top of the second inning of a 7-5 victory at Reading. Fulton catches the final eight innings, allowing five steals and three passed balls. He also drills pitcher **Heath Haynes** (1992-93) in the chest with a throw on Ron Lockett's steal of second base in the seventh. The next would-be throw to second, which Fulton wisely holds, has Haynes diving for the dirt rather than taking another shot to the sternum.

2001: For the third straight season, the Senators bunt into a triple play, this one off the bat of pitcher **Mark Mangum** (2001-02) in the second inning of a 7-4 victory at Altoona.

May 3

1884: Hall of Fame pitcher **Chief Bender** (1902) born in Crow Wing County, Minn.

1989: Reading's Jason Grimsley no-hits the Senators 3-0 in the first game of a double-header on City Island.

May 4

2001: Baseball America names the 1993 Senators – the juggernaut that wins 100 games and the Eastern League title – as the 73rd best team in the century-old history of the minors.

May 5

2003: Utility player **Matt Stairs** (1991), playing for the Pirates, launches a pitch from Astros' Wade Miller deep into the right-field seats – a 461-foot shot that is the longest homer ever at Minute Maid Park. Stairs' homer in the eighth inning accounts for the Pirates' only run in an 8-1 loss.

May 6

1971: Infielder **Izzy Alcantara** (1995-97) born in Bani, D.R.

1998: Outfielder **Moises Alou** (1989-90) strikes out three times at Wrigley Field, but he has plenty of company on the Astros as Cubs rookie Kerry Wood ties a major league record with 20 strikeouts in a nine-inning game.

May 7

1997: Shortstop **Mike Lansing** (1992) homers twice and drives in five runs in the sixth inning alone as the Expos score 13 runs en route to a 19-3 victory at San Francisco. The 13 runs are the most ever scored in the sixth inning of a National League game.

May 8

1906: Hall of Fame pitcher **Chief Bender** (1902) plays left field for the injury-depleted A's and homers twice – both inside the park – off Jesse Tannehill in an 11-4 win at Boston.

1917: Catcher **Harry O'Neill** (1940), one of two former major leaguers killed in World War II, born in Philadelphia.

1964: Despite tornado warnings near Cleveland, future pitching coach **Tommy John** (2002) starts for the Indians against the Yankees. He lasts just five batters, one of whom – Mickey Mantle – drills a three-run homer for a quick 3-0 lead that turns into a 10-3 rout.

1981: Manager **Eddie Onslow** (1931-33) dies in Dennison, Ohio, at age 88.

May 9

1969: First baseman **Desi Wilson** (2002) born in Glen Cove, N.Y.

1988: Future pitching coach **Jerry Reuss** (2000), then with the White Sox, collects his 200th career victory in a 3-0 shutout at Baltimore.

1991: Pitcher **Ian Krol** (2013) born in Hinsdale, Ill.

1994: Pitcher **Ugueth Urbina** (1993-94) temporarily leaves the Senators after his father, Juan, is killed during a robbery in Caracas, Venz.

1995: First baseman **Shawn Gallagher** (2000), playing scholastically for New Hanover High in Wilmington, N.C., is hitless before being intentionally walked in his final at-bat to end a 51-game hitting streak, tying the high school record set by Stan Brown of Noblesville, Ind.

PAUL DEMNY

1999: After missing a hit-and-run sign, **Tim Cossins** (1999) bunts into a triple play with **Andy Tracy** (1998-99) and **Jon Tucker** (1998-99) running on the play in the second inning of a 6-4 victory over Binghamton on City Island.

2002: First baseman **Desi Wilson** (2002) has his 33rd birthday spoiled as the Expos release him from the Senators' roster.

2013: Paul Demny (2012-13) and **Ian Krol** (2013) combine for the fourth no-hitter of Senators' modern era in a 6-1 victory at Binghamton. Demny allows an unearned run in the seventh inning and leaves after eight as his pitch count reaches 113. Krol needs only 10 pitches in the ninth to finish the game.

IAN KROL

May 10

1894: Infielder **Doggie Miller** (1893), then playing with St. Louis, sandwiches a home run between ones by Frank Shugart and Heinie Peitz in the seventh inning against Cincinnati, marking the first time three teammates hit consecutive homers. The Reds still win 18-9.

DOGGIE MILLER

   1985: Pitcher **Luis Atilano** (2008-09, 2011) born in Santurce, P.R.

   1995: The Eastern League approves plans by the Senators' owners – a quartet of investors from suburban Philadelphia – to move the franchise to Springfield, Mass., following the 1996 season. The move never happens as Harrisburg mayor **Stephen Reed** appeals to the National Association, which gives the city a chance to purchase the team.

   2012: Vladimir Guerrero (1996) signs a minor league deal with Toronto, raising expectations he will soon return to the majors. Alas, Guerrero is soon released, despite hitting .358 in 12 games with four homers and 12 RBIs for Toronto's Class A and AAA teams.

May 11

   2004: Longtime minor league owner **David Hersh** backs out of a $9.4 million deal to buy the Senators, leaving the city of Harrisburg with a team it has owned since 1995.

May 12

   1910: A's pitcher **Chief Bender** (1902) no-hits Cleveland 4-0 at Shibe Park.

   1987: The Senators lose their 11th straight game, a modern franchise record for futility that lasts until 2009. The skid ends the next game with a 7-2 victory over Williamsport on City Island.

   2010: Outfielder **Roger Bernadina** (2007-08) hits his first two homers in the majors as the Nationals beat the Mets 6-4 at Citi Field.

May 13

   2009: Third baseman **Ryan Zimmerman** (2005) picks up two walks but goes 0-for-3 in the Nationals' 6-3 victory at San Francisco to snap his hitting streak at 30 games – one game shy of matching the franchise record set in 1999 by **Vladimir Guerrero** (1996).

May 14

   1963: Outfielder **Ben Abner** (1987) born in Mechanicsburg, Pa.

   2000: Third baseman **Jason Camilli** (1998-2000) commits a franchise-record five errors during the Senators' 6-4 victory over Binghamton on City Island.

   2006: Outfielder **Jim Lemon** (1949) dies in Brandon, Miss., at age 78.

   2012: Catcher **Sandy Leon** (2012-13) makes his major league debut, starting for the Nationals against San Diego and going 0-for-1 before suffering a high ankle sprain in the top of the fourth inning. He misses the next two months of the season.

May 15
1888: Manager **Steve Yerkes** (1924) born in Hatboro, Pa.

1976: Outfielder **Dan McKinley** (2000, 2002) born in Phoenix, Ariz.

1994: New Haven piles up 14 runs in the fifth inning off pitchers **Bob Baxter** (1994) and **Terry Powers** (1994) en route to a 22-2 flogging of the Senators on City Island.

May 16
1906: Hall of Fame pitcher **Vic Willis** (1895) tosses his first of three straight shutouts for the Pirates, beating the New York Giants 4-0 at Pittsburgh's Exposition Park.

1994: Closer **Al Reyes** (1994) starts the Senators' first triple play in their modern era to clinch a 5-3 victory over Bowie on City Island. Reyes first snares Bo Ortiz's low liner up the middle before throwing to **Mike Hardge** (1993-94), who tags second to double up Brent Miller before relaying to first baseman **Randy Wilstead** (1993-94) to catch Hector Vargas and complete the triple play.

AL REYES

1995: The Senators introduce new mascot Uncle Slam over a handful of finalists that include Slammin' Sam, Senator Phil-A-Buster and Susquehanna Sam the Dancin' Man. Slam's stay lasts eight years before the arrival of a multi-colored carpet remnant with legs, arms and an oversized head named Rascal.

1998: Pitcher **Mike Johnson** (1998) begins a dizzying 48 hours in which he flies from Harrisburg to Los Angeles, where he stays long enough to start the Expos' 6-3 loss at Dodger Stadium before jetting back to Montreal and then on to Harrisburg. A day later, the Expos send Johnson from Harrisburg to Class AAA Ottawa, completing a two-day trek of 5,542 miles.

2007: Twelve years after buying the Senators to keep them from moving to Springfield, Mass., the city of Harrisburg agrees to sell the team to **Michael Reinsdorf** – the son of White Sox owner Jerry Reinsdorf. The $13.25 million price tag is a record for an Eastern League team and nearly twice what the city paid for the franchise after the 1995 season.

May 17
1993: Second baseman **Ron Krause** (1993) retires, creating an opening for second baseman **Mike Hardge** (1993-94) to join the Senators from Class A West Palm Beach.

May 18
1912: Detroit manager **Hughie Jennings** (1890) recruits replacement players after the Tigers go on strike in support of suspended outfielder Ty Cobb. To keep from forfeiting the day's game at Shibe Park against the Philadelphia Athletics, Jennings puts together a team of local college and semipro players, and loses 24-2.

May 19

1996: The Eastern League's oldest player and one of its youngest – 30-year-old **Charlie Montoyo** (1996) and 21-year-old **Vladimir Guerrero** (1996) – drive in three runs in the Senators' 3-1 victory over Binghamton on City Island. Guerrero hits a two-run homer in the first inning while Montoyo's sixth-inning single scores Guerrero for the Senators' third run.

May 20

2011: Infielder **Danny Espinosa** (2010) drives in five runs in the Nationals' 17-5 rout of the Orioles at Camden Yards.

JEFF KING

May 21

1919: Outfielder **Jim Thorpe** (1915) is claimed by the Boston Braves from the New York Giants for $1,500 in what will be his sixth and final season in the majors.

1962: Outfielder **Bernie Tatis** (1989) born in Villa Vasquez, D.R.

2013: Pitcher-outfielder **Cot Deal** (1942) dies in Oklahoma City at age 90.

May 22

1943: Pitching coach **Tommy John** (2002) born in Terre Haute, Ind.

1954: Hall of Fame pitcher **Chief Bender** (1902) dies in Philadelphia at age 70.

1974: Catcher **Jason Brown** (2002-04) born in Long Beach, Calif.

2010: Matt Stairs (1991) homers for the Padres in a 2-1 win at Seattle, marking the 11th different franchise for which Stairs homers – tying Todd Zeile's major league record.

May 23

1986: Pitcher **Jordan Zimmermann** (2008, 2010) born in Auburndale, Wis.

1993: A 9-2 victory over London on City Island is interrupted by a seventh-inning, bench-clearing brawl that starts when reliever Brian Warren throws a pitch over the head of **Mike Hardge** (1993-94) after giving up back-to-back homers to **Cliff Floyd** (1993) and **Oreste Marrero** (1993).

1999: Third baseman **Jeff King** (1987-88), then with Kansas City, says he no longer is interested in playing and retires.

2007: Trailing 7-0 with one out in the ninth inning, the Senators rally on City Island to tie the score before beating Erie 8-7 on a 10th-inning sacrifice fly by **Melvin Dorta** (2004-07). The ninth-inning comeback is the largest in modern franchise history.

2011: Nationals outfielder **Rick Ankiel** (2011) begins an injury rehab assignment for the Senators in a most inglorious way, striking out in all four of his at-bats during a 12-8 loss at Akron. Ankiel returns to Washington the next day.

May 24
1951: Manager **Dave Machemer** (2003-04) born in St. Joseph, Mich.

1965: Hitting coach **Rob Ducey** (2004) born in Toronto.

1976: Third baseman **Brandon Larson** (2007) born in San Angelo, Tex.

1995: The Expos trade pitcher **Joey Eischen** (1993) and outfielder Roberto Kelly to the Dodgers for outfielder Henry Rodriguez and infielder Jeff Treadway.

May 25
1970: Pitcher **Joey Eischen** (1993) born in West Covina, Calif.

1979: Pitcher **Chris Young** (2003) born in Dallas, Tex.

May 26
1987: The Pirates trade outfielder **Ben Abner** (1987) to St. Louis for first baseman **Ron**

Johns (1987-88) in a move that helps propel the Senators to the 1987 Eastern League title.

1988: With a then-record crowd of 5,088 watching, the Pirates beat the Senators 5-2 in an exhibition game on City Island. The Pirates also extend their working agreement with the Senators through 1990, which turns out to be the last year of the affiliation.

1995: First baseman **Frank Jacobs** (1995), whose ninth-inning homer topped the Senators in the pivotal Game 3 of the 1994 Eastern League finals, is acquired by the Expos from the Mets for pitcher **Darrin Paxton** (1994-95) and assigned to Harrisburg.

BEN ABNER

May 27
1937: Hall of Fame infielder **Frank Grant** (1890) dies in New York City at age 71.

2008: Indians infielder **Jamey Carroll** (1998-2000, 2002) is part of a rare triple steal. When White Sox pitcher Ehren Wasserman tries to pick off Carroll from first base, David Dellucci breaks from third base and scores ahead of the throw home by Chicago first baseman Paul Konerko. As Dellucci scores, Grady Sizemore goes from second to third while Carroll moves into second with the third steal of the play.

NATE KARNS

May 28
1887: Outfielder **Jim Thorpe** (1915) born in Prague, Okla.

2013: Pitcher **Nate Karns** (2013) is plucked from City Island to Washington, where he joins the Nationals for his major league debut – but not first without waiting out an 81-minute rain delay. Karns allows three runs on five hits during his 85-pitch start against Baltimore, but does not qualify for the win as he leaves the game with one out in the fifth inning of the Nationals' 9-3 victory.

May 29

1959: With President Dwight Eisenhower among the crowd of only 3,030 at Griffith Stadium, left fielder **Jim Lemon** (1949) goes 2-for-3 with a double and homer in the Washington Senators' 7-6 victory over the Red Sox.

1992: Future hitting coach **Tim Raines Sr.** (2007) steals two bases in the White Sox's 3-0 loss at Toronto, giving him 700 stolen bases en route to 808 in his career – a total that ranks fifth all-time behind Hall of Famers Rickey Henderson, Lou Brock, onetime Harrisburg player-manager **Billy Hamilton** (1905-06) and Ty Cobb.

1993: The Senators beat Albany-Colonie 8-2 for a modern franchise-record 12th straight victory. The streak ends the next day with an 8-2 loss to the New York Yankees' Eastern League affiliate.

1999: Norwich catcher Victor Valencia hits three homers before the Senators rally to score twice in the ninth inning for an 11-10 victory on City Island.

JIM LEMON

May 30

1956: Playing right field for Washington, **Jim Lemon** (1949) has a perfect view to one of the more awe-inspiring moments in the career of Mickey Mantle, who drills a fifth-inning pitch from Pedro Ramos off the top of the façade above the third deck in old Yankee Stadium. Mantle comes within 18 inches of being the first player to hit a ball completely out of Yankee Stadium. Accounting for trajectory, team officials estimate Mantle's drive – had it not struck the façade – would have traveled 525 feet.

1990: Outfielder **Eury Perez** (2012) born in San Luis, D.R.

1998: A crowd of 6,676 – then the largest ever to watch a game at RiverSide Stadium – sees the Senators beat Bowie 2-1.

1999: In a preview of what is to be, **Jon Tucker** (1998-99) drills a two-out, two-strike, ninth-inning grand slam off Norwich closer Joe Lisio to lift the Senators to a 9-5 victory on City Island. Less than four months later, **Milton Bradley** (1999) does the same to Lisio with another two-out, two-strike, ninth-inning grand slam to beat the Navigators 12-11 on City Island and give the Senators an Eastern League-record fourth straight title.

May 31

1998: A three-run, pinch-hit homer in the eighth inning by Ryan Minor carries Bowie over the Senators 5-4 to a start horrific slide in which Harrisburg loses 24 of 29 games before recovering in time to win a third straight Eastern League title.

2006: Pitcher **Billy Sylvester** (2005-06) walks a modern franchise-record 11 batters in only five innings of the Senators' 9-0 loss in the second game of a doubleheader at New Britain.

June 1

1937: Pitcher **Bill "Bullfrog" Dietrich** (1931) tosses a no-hitter for the Chicago White Sox, beating the St. Louis Browns 8-0 at Comiskey Park.

1977: Outfielder **Brad Wilkerson** (1999-2000) born in Owensboro, Ky.

2004: The Senators play the longest game in their modern era, going 16 innings before falling 4-3 to Trenton on City Island.

2007: Bowie's Radhames Liz strikes out eight while no-hitting the Senators 5-0 at Prince George's Stadium.

BILL DIETRICH

June 2

1970: Pitcher **Reid Cornelius** (1991-93) born in Thomasville, Ala.

2010: Armando Galarraga (2005) seems to have pitched a perfect game for the Detroit Tigers, but first-base umpire Jim Joyce inexplicably calls Cleveland's Jason Donald safe on an infield single with two outs in the ninth inning. Replays clearly show Donald is out. Galarraga then retires Trevor Crowe on another grounder to complete a 3-0 shutout.

June 3

1907: Pitcher **Ulysses Simpson Grant McGlynn** (1901) starts both ends of St. Louis' doubleheader at Cincinnati, winning the opener 1-0 before losing the second game 5-1.

2010: Four days before being picked first overall by the Nationals in the amateur draft, catcher-turned-outfielder **Bryce Harper** (2011, 2013), then 17 years old and playing for Southern Nevada, ends his college career by being ejected in the Junior College World

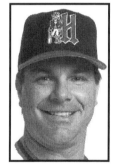

Series and receiving a two-game suspension for arguing with an umpire over the strike zone.

June 4

1975: The first round of the amateur draft sees future Senators manager **Rick Sofield** (1997), then a high school outfielder from Morristown. N.J. taken by Minnesota with the 13th overall pick out with future pitching coach **Bo McLaughlin** (1995-96) following at No. 14 to Houston out of David Lipscomb College in Tennessee.

1984: The Mets select Mechanicsburg High outfielder **Shawn Abner** with the first overall pick of the amateur draft.

RICK SOFIELD

1999: Unbeknownst to most in the Expos' organization, Senators manager **Doug Sisson** (1999-2000) contacts the legendary Ron Polk about joining his staff at the University of Georgia. Polk interviews Sisson by telephone and hires him, leading to Sisson's sudden resignation a month later as the Senators' manager – a resignation that is brief as Sisson quickly changes his mind and asks the Expos to let him return to Harrisburg.

2010: Manager **Dave Trembley** (1987-89) is fired by Baltimore after a 15-39 start in his fourth season leading the Orioles.

June 5

1952: Bob Berresford (1952) no-hits Wilmington 1-0 in a nine-inning game, the last no-hitter on City Island until Binghamton's Bill Pulsipher stymies the Senators 2-0 in Game 2 of the 1994 Eastern League finals.

1994: Playing on a field suited better for Wiffle Ball than baseball, the Senators fall 28-10 to Bowie at the University of Maryland's undersized Shipley Field.

2003: Pitcher **Pat Collins** (2002-03) gives a one-finger salute to a boisterous fan along the first-base line while leaving during the Senators' 11-8 victory over New Britain on City Island. For his gesture, Collins receives a six-game suspension.

2012: Shortstop **Ian Desmond** (2006, 2008-09) drives in the game-tying run in the eighth inning and then again in the 10th and 12th before Washington finally beats the Mets 7-6 in 12 innings at Nationals Park.

June 6

1931: Bill "Bullfrog" Dietrich (1931) no-hits Wilkes-Barre 1-0 in a nine-inning game.

1979: Outfielder **Jesus Feliciano** (2005-06) born in Bayamon, P.R.

1990: Infielder **Anthony Rendon** (2012-13) born in Richmond, Tex.

June 7

1930: Pitcher **Bob Berresford** (1952) born in West William Penn, Pa.

1973: After Texas makes high school pitcher David Clyde the first overall draft choice, the Phillies select catcher and future Senators manager **John Stearns** (2006, 2008-09) – just before the Brewers and Padres take future Hall of Famers Robin Yount and Dave Winfield.

1986: The Pirates pick University of Arkansas third baseman **Jeff King** (1987-88) with the first pick of the amateur draft.

1997: A then-record crowd of 6,583 on City Island sees a 4-2 victory over New Haven.

1998: Harrisburg native and former major league pitcher Tom Buskey dies in Harrisburg, Pa., at age 51.

2000: Reading's Pete Zamora throws a perfect game – the fifth in Eastern League history – to beat the Senators 6-0 in the second game of a doubleheader at Municipal Stadium.

2010: The Nationals select catcher-turned-outfielder **Bryce Harper** (2011, 2013) with the first overall pick of the amateur draft.

June 8

1912: Pitcher **Lew Krausse** (1933-35) born in Media, Pa.

1963: Outfielder-turned-pitcher **Scott Ruskin** (1988-89) born in Jacksonville, Fla.

2005: Pitcher **Ugueth Urbina** (1993-94) is traded, along with infielder Ramon Martinez, from the Detroit Tigers to the Phillies for second baseman Placido Polanco.

2010: After opening the season in Harrisburg, pitcher **Stephen Strasburg** (2010-11) makes his debut in the majors, striking out 14 and walking none in seven innings of Washington's 4-2 win over the Pirates before a sell-out crowd of 40,315 at Nationals Park.

June 9

1997: Frustrated with a 13-2 loss to lowly New Haven, manager **Rick Sofield** (1997) uses an off day before the All-Star break to put the Eastern League-leading Senators through an early morning workout on City Island.

1999: Relief pitcher **Guillermo Mota** (1998) hits a three-run homer in his first at-bat in the majors as the Expos crush Boston 13-1 during an interleague game in Montreal.

GUILLERMO MOTA

June 10

1901: Pitcher **Vic Willis** (1895) hits the only homer of his Hall of Fame career as the Boston Beaneaters win 9-5 at Cincinnati.

1912: Chief Meyers (1906) becomes the first catcher in history to hit for the cycle in the New York Giants' 9-8 loss to the Cubs at the Polo Grounds.

1973: Pitcher **Julio Manon** (2000-02) born in Guerra, D.R.

1983: Pitcher **Matt Chico** (2006, 2009-11) born in Fullerton, Calif.

1998: With **Shayne Bennett** (1996-97) pitching, longtime Expos outfielder and future Senators hitting coach **Tim Raines** (2007) returns to Montreal and steals the 800th base of his Hall of Fame-caliber career during the Yankees' 6-2 victory at Olympic Stadium.

2010: Starter **Chuck James** (2010) combines with **Cole Kimball** (2010, 2012) and **Zech Zinicola** (2006-12) to no-hit Altoona 1-0 in the second game of a doubleheader at Blair County Ballpark.

GENE MOORE

June 11

1938: Three former Senators – **Gene Moore** (1932), **Elbie Fletcher** (1934) and **Ray Mueller** (1932-34) – take turns batting out of the leadoff spot for Boston but end up going 0-for-3 with a walk at Crosley Field as the Reds' Johnny Vander Meer beats the Braves 3-0 in the first of his record back-to-back, no-hitters. Four days later, Vander Meer no-hits Brooklyn 6-0 in the first night game at Ebbets Field. His shortstop for both games is **Billy Meyers** of Enola, Pa.

1995: Expos center fielder **Rondell White** (1992-93, 1996) collects six hits to join Tim Foli, Chris Speier and **Tim Raines** (2007) as the only Expos to this point to hit for the cycle in a 10-8, 13-inning victory over the Giants in Montreal.

2005: Outfielder **Dermal Brown** (2005) hits three homers, including the game winner in the 12th inning, as the Senators beat Reading 6-5 on City Island. Brown joins **Ron Johns** (1987-88) and **Bob Natal** (1991) as the only modern-era Senators to homer three times in a game.

June 12

1984: Outfielder **Roger Bernadina** (2007-08) born in Willemstad, Curacao.

1987: Jeff Cook (1987-90) hits into a triple play as his sinking liner to left field in the fifth inning is caught by Pittsfield's Dwight Smith, who then starts a relay of throws to catch **Dimas Gutierrez** (1987-88) and **Tom Prince** (1987) wandering off base. The Cubs win 6-3 in 10 innings on City Island.

1999: Less than three weeks shy of his 32nd birthday, third baseman **John Wehner** (1990) returns to City Island as a utility player-surrogate coach for Altoona and steals home on the back end of a double steal in a 4-2 victory over the Senators. Wehner's steal of home is his first since 1990, when he did it five times for the Senators – all on double steals.

June 13

1973: Future pitching coach **Tommy John** (2002) gives up eight runs before leaving in the second inning of the Dodgers' 16-3 loss at Philadelphia in a game that marks the first time Los Angeles puts together the infield of first baseman Steve Garvey, second baseman Davey Lopes, shortstop Bill Russell and third baseman Ron Cey – a quartet that plays together for the next 8 ½ seasons, the longest such run for any infield in history.

June 14

1966: Pitcher **Randy Tomlin** (1989-90) born in Bainbridge, Md.

1978: Infielder **Edgar Gonzalez** (2005) born in San Diego.

2011: A one-out single in the eighth inning by Cleveland shortstop **Orlando Cabrera** (1997) breaks up a bid by Detroit's Justin Verlander for a second career no-hitter in the Tigers' 4-0 victory.

June 15

1978: Pitcher **Zach Day** (2005) born in Cincinnati, Ohio.

June 16

1909: Outfielder **Jim Thorpe** (1915) makes his pro pitching debut for Rocky Mount in a 4-2 victory over Raleigh in the Eastern Carolina League.

2011: Pitcher **Cliff Lee** (2002) has as many hits – two – as he allows in the Phillies' 3-0 shutout of the Marlins in Philadelphia. He follows with shutouts in his next two starts against the Cardinals and Red Sox to become the first Phillies pitcher with three straight shutouts since Hall of Famer Robin Roberts in 1950.

June 17

1978: Infielder **Dan DeMent** (2005-07) born in Palos Heights, Ill.

1987: First baseman **Ron Johns** (1987-88) goes 6-for-6 with three homers, three singles and nine RBIs as the Senators rout Albany-Colonie 26-9 on City Island.

June 17 (continued)

1997: The Senators hold the first of their annual Negro League Nights to honor the Harrisburg Giants of the mid-1920s.

2001: Two years before joining the Senators, **Blake Stein** (2003) strikes out eight straight batters in Kansas City's 5-2 loss to Milwaukee as he joins Nolan Ryan, Ron Davis and Roger Clemens as the only American League pitchers to ever strike out eight batters in a row.

2007: Outfielder **Brandon Watson** (2002-03, 2005), then playing for Class AAA Columbus, singles off Ottawa's J.D. Durbin in the sixth inning to extend his hitting streak to 43 games, breaking the International League record set by Rochester's Jack Lelivelt in 1912.

2007: Pitcher **Micah Bowie** (2005) allows only two runs over the first six innings of the Nationals' 4-2 victory at Toronto. One of those runs comes on a solo homer in the third inning by Frank Thomas, whose drive to deep left-center is his 244th homer as a designated hitter to break the DH career record set by Seattle's Edgar Martinez.

DAVE TREMBLEY

June 18

1992: General manager **Rick Redd** (1987-92) leaves the Senators to accept a position overseeing the expansion Florida Marlins' minor league complex in Viera, Fla. Assistant GM **Todd Vander Woude** (1987-2007) is promoted to fill Redd's position.

1999: Decimated by injuries, the Senators have only eight position players and a DH available for their doubleheader against Trenton on City Island. The Senators win both games, 8-6 and 3-0.

2006: **Dan DeMent** (2005-07) and **Tim Raines Jr.** (2006) each hit two homers while the Senators slam a modern franchise-record eight in a 17-8 victory at Erie.

2007: After two decades of riding the back roads in the minors, manager **Dave Trembley** (1987-89) is named the Orioles' manager after Sam Perlozzo is fired. Trembley keeps the job until early in the 2010 season.

DAN DeMENT

2009: Pitcher **Craig Stammen** (2008) and the Nationals wait out a five-hour rain delay in the Bronx before beating the Yankees 3-0 in a game that marks two firsts – Stammen's first victory in the majors and the first homerless game at the new Yankee Stadium.

2010: Pitcher **Stephen Strasburg** (2010-11) strikes out 10 White Sox batters in seven innings, giving him 32 strikeouts in his first three starts in the majors and breaking the previous mark of 29 set by the Astros' J.R. Richard in 1971. Strasburg, though, receives a no-decision as Chicago beats Washington 2-1 in 11 innings at Nationals Park.

June 19

1944: Five days after his 18th birthday – and five years before reaching the major leagues with Brooklyn – first-year pro Don Newcombe of the Newark Eagles beats Josh Gibson and the Homestead Grays 9-2 in a Negro League game before a crowd of 2,500 on City Island. The victory is Newcombe's first in a pro career that includes a 10-year stay in the majors, where he will be named rookie of the year and MVP as well as a Cy Young Award winner.

1949: Pitching coach **Jerry Reuss** (2000) born in St. Louis, Mo.

1978: Pitcher **Claudio Vargas** (2002-03) born in Mao, D.R.

June 20

1978: Pitcher **Bill "Bullfrog" Dietrich** (1931) dies in Philadelphia at age 68.

June 21

1952: The financially strapped and last-place Senators offer a player's contract to ste-

nographer-turned-shortstop **Eleanor Engle**, who works out the next day on City Island before her contract is voided by minor league president George Trautman.

1978: Future Harrisburg manager **Dave Machemer** (2003-04) becomes the first player in history to homer while leading off the game in his major league debut. Machemer's moment comes for the Angels against the Twins' Geoff Zahn at Minneapolis' Metropolitan Stadium, where he deposits Zahn's 3-2 fastball into the left-field seats to start the Angels' 5-2 victory. The homer turns out to be the only one in Machemer's brief stay in

DAVE MACHEMER

the majors, a career that lasts only 55 plate appearances over two seasons.

1999: The Senators win 5-4 at Portland, but the victory is forfeited after a clerical error leads manager **Doug Sisson** (1999-2000) to inadvertently use an ineligible player, infielder **David Post** (1997-99), who has not yet been officially added to the roster.

June 22

1949: Pitching coach **Dave Tomlin** (1994) born in Maysville, Ky.

1978: Pitcher **Anthony Ferrari** (2002-05) born in San Francis-co.

1990: With President George H. Bush – No. 41, not Dubya – in attendance, the Senators fall 6-3 at Hagerstown.

2013: The 1931 road gray uniform worn by manager **Eddie Onslow** (1931-33) is the centerpiece of the Senators' 27th annual auction to benefit United Cerebral Palsy. The one-of-a-kind item, though, sells for only $1,100 – barely half of the $2,000 UCP spends a few months earlier to acquire the uniform with the hope of flipping it for far more at its annual midseason auction on City Island.

EDDIE ONSLOW

June 23

2010: Pitcher **Stephen Strasburg** (2010-11) strikes out nine in only six innings, giving him 41 strikeouts in his first four starts, but loses 1-0 to Kansas City at Nationals Park.

June 24

1994: Pitcher **Rafael Diaz** (1993-95) proposes to girlfriend Xiomara Barillas on the field after she throws out the ceremonial first pitch before a 6-3 win over Portland on City Island.

2003: Outfielder **Brad Wilkerson** (1999-2000) hits for the cycle and drives in four runs as the Expos beat the Pirates 6-4 at Olympic Stadium. Wilkerson puts together another cycle less than two years later – after the Expos leave Montreal for Washington.

2003: The Senators scrub a "Vladimir Gorilla" bobblehead promotion after the real **Vladimir Guerrero** (1996) objects to being depicted as a primate.

June 25

1949: First baseman and two-time major league home run leader **Buck Freeman** (1910) dies in Wilkes-Barre, Pa., at age 77.

2005: Less than a month after being the fourth overall pick of the amateur draft, third baseman **Ryan Zimmerman** (2005) makes his Class AA debut on City Island and picks up three hits in an 8-6 victory over Akron. He quickly emerges as one of the best prospects to play on the island, batting .326 in 63 games for the Senators before ending the season in the majors with Washington.

BUCK FREEMAN

June 26

1928: The New York Yankees and Senators play to a 6-6 tie in an exhibition game on City Island, where Babe Ruth launches a pitch from **Johnny Tillman** (1928-30) into the second row of trees beyond the right-field fence.

June 27

1980: Future pitching coach **Jerry Reuss** (2000), then with the Dodgers, no-hits the Giants 8-0 in San Francisco.

1988: The Nationals beat the Americans 6-0 in the Eastern League All-Star Game played before a crowd of 2,878 on City Island.

2002: In the worst trade of their 35-year existence, the Expos give top prospects and future All-Stars **Brandon Phillips** (2001-02), **Cliff Lee** (2002) and outfielder Grady Sizemore, along with first baseman Lee Stevens, to Cleveland for starting pitcher Bartolo Colon and journeyman reliever Tim Drew.

2013: Nationals outfielder and 2012 National League rookie of the year **Bryce Harper** (2011, 2013) rejoins the Senators in Bowie to continue his injury rehab assignment for bursitis in his left knee and goes 2-for-4 with a two-run triple in an 11-6 victory. He returns to the Nationals four days later and, after missing 31 games, homers off Milwaukee's Yovani Gallardo in his first at-bat of a 10-5 victory in Washington.

June 28

1981: Infielder **Brandon Phillips** (2001-02) born in Raleigh, N.C.

June 29

1967: Third baseman **John Wehner** (1990) born in Pittsburgh.

1980: Pitcher **Seung Song** (2002-03) born in Pusan, South Korea.

1994: Catcher **Ray Mueller** (1932-34) dies in Lower Paxton Township, Pa., at age 82.

2000: Catcher **Scott Sandusky** (2000-03) bunts into a triple play in the seventh inning of the Senators' 4-0 win at Bowie.

2000: The Yankees trade pitchers **Jake Westbrook** (1999) and **Zach Day** (2005), and outfielder Ricky Ledee, to the Indians for outfielder David Justice.

2013: After a 7-0 start for the Senators, **Taylor Jordan** (2013) makes his major league debut, allowing only one earned run over 4 1/3 innings in the Nationals' 5-1 loss to the Mets at Citi Field.

June 30

1909: Fourteen years after making his pro debut on City Island, Hall of Fame pitcher **Vic Willis** (1895) opens Pittsburgh's Forbes Field, starting the first game there as the Pirates lose to the Chicago Cubs 3-2.

VIC WILLIS

1970: Shortstop **Mark Grudzielanek** (1994) born in Milwaukee.

1988: Infielder-outfielder **Jeff Kobernus** (2012) born in San Leandro, Calif.

2013: Knuckleball-happy pitcher Eddie Gamboa of the Bowie Baysox no-hits the Senators 7-0 in a seven-inning game at Prince George's Stadium – marking the first time the Senators have been no-hit since June 1, 2007 at Bowie, where the Baysox's Radhames Liz shut them down 5-0.

July 1

1888: Harrisburg Giants Hall of Fame first baseman **Ben Taylor** (1925) born in Anderson, S.C.

2000: In a rare matchup of Canadian starting pitchers – and coinciding with Canada's 133rd birthday – Montreal's **Mike Johnson** (1998) finds himself on the losing end of a 6-5 decision to Florida's **Ryan Dempster** at Olympic Stadium.

2005: Major League Baseball suspends infielder **Ramon Castro** (2005) a record 105 games for possessing amphetamines with intent to distribute. Shortstop **Josh Labandeira** (2003-05) also receives a 15-game ban for possessing, but not using, amphetamines.

July 2

1972: Pitcher-manager **Rankin Johnson** (1925-26) dies in Williamsport, Pa., at 84.

1988: First baseman **Chris Marrero** (2009-10, 2012) born in Miami, Fla.

July 3

1966: Outfielder **Moises Alou** (1989-90) born in Atlanta.

1975: Pitcher **Christian Parker** (1998-99) born in Albuquerque, N.M.

1987: Pitcher **Brett Gideon** (1987-88) becomes the first of the modern-era Senators to be promoted to the majors as he joins the Pirates.

2001: Infielder **Izzy Alcantara** (1995-97), then with Class AAA Pawtucket, earns national headlines for all the wrong reasons as he reacts to an inside pitch from Scranton/Wilkes-Barre's Blas Cedeno by kicking catcher Jeremy Salazar in the chest before charging the mound. The International League suspends Alcantara for seven games before Boston promotes him to the majors on Sept. 1.

July 4

1993: Center fielder **Rondell White** (1992-93, 1996) sees his hitting streak for the Senators end at 24 games, capping a 45-for-105 run over which his batting average jumps to .331 and makes a distant memory of an 8-for-75 slump that starts his season.

2003: Center fielder **Brandon Watson** (2002-03, 2005) becomes the second Senator of the modern era – first baseman **Ron Johns** (1987-88) being the first – to pick up six hits in a game during a 12-8 victory at Akron. Watson's hits are all singles.

2011: Highly touted and equally hyped teenager **Bryce Harper** (2011, 2013), the top pick in the 2010 amateur draft, arrives on City Island, starts in left field and goes 2-for-3 in his Senators debut

during an 8-1 victory over Erie before a then-franchise record crowd of 8,092. Harper, three months shy of his 19th birthday, becomes Harrisburg's youngest player since 18-year-old **Bob Keller** played second base in 1935.

July 5

1970: Pitcher **Doug Bochtler** (1992) born in West Palm Beach, Fla.

1983: Pitcher **Marco Estrada** (2008) born in Sonora, Mex.

1999: Manager **Doug Sisson** (1999-2000) abruptly quits to accept a job as an assistant coach at the University of Georgia. On his way out of town, Sisson blasts the fans and media. A week later – and only after pleading with the Expos for a second chance – Sisson contritely returns to Harrisburg and publicly apologizes for his boorish behavior.

2001: Switch-hitting infielder **Geoff Blum** (1996, 1998) homers from each side of the plate in his first two at-bats during the Expos' 9-6 victory over the Marlins in Montreal.

July 6

1966: Pitcher **Darrin Winston** (1993-94) born in Passaic, N.J.

July 7

1983: Catcher **Luke Montz** (2007-09) born in Lafayette, La.

1937: Outfielder **Gene Moore** (1932), then with the Boston Braves, becomes the first former Harrisburg player selected to the major league all-star game, but does not play in the National League's 8-3 loss at Washington's Griffith Stadium.

1993: Pitcher **Kirk Rueter** (1993) makes his major league debut in Montreal and works into the ninth inning before John Wetteland gets the final two outs in a 3-0 victory over the San Francisco Giants.

1995: To keep the team's owners from relocating the Senators to Springfield, Mass., Harrisburg mayor **Stephen Reed** completes a deal for the city to buy the franchise for $6.7 million – a record price for a Class AA franchise. Only six months earlier, the previous owners paid $4.1 million for the franchise.

2008: The Senators hire **Kevin Kulp** as team president.

2010: Utility player **Matt Stairs** (1991), playing with San Diego, launches a ninth-inning, pinch-hit homer off Nationals closer Matt Capps in a 7-6 loss in Washington. The homer is Stairs' 20th as a pinch-hitter, tying the major league record set by Cliff Johnson.

July 8

1988: Kris Roth no-hits the Senators 3-0 at Pittsfield.

1994: Longtime minor league operator William Collins III agrees to buy the Senators for $3.5 million from owner **Jerry Mileur**, who 10 weeks later backs out of the deal to sell the team for $4.1 million to a quartet of investors from suburban Philadelphia.

1999: Outfielders **Peter Bergeron** (1998-99) and **Milton Bradley** (1999) are selected to represent the United States in the upcoming Pan-Am Games. Outfielder **Jeremy Ware** (1999-2004) also wins a roster spot on Team Canada.

July 9

1901: Pitcher **Lou Polli** (1927) born in Baveno, Italy.

1946: Sore-armed pitcher **Max Patkin** begins his five-decade career as the "Clown Prince of Baseball" when he performs during the Cleveland Indians' exhibition game against the Senators on City Island.

1993: Outfielder **Moises Alou** (1989-90) hits two homers off San Diego's Tim Wor-rell in the Expos' 6-1 victory over the Padres at Olympic Stadium, giving him six homers

Max Patkin back on the island in 1988

on his last six hits – a major league record that takes Alou four games to accomplish.

2010: For the fourth time in less than a year, pitcher **Cliff Lee** (2002) changes team. This time, Lee – who had been with the Indians and Phillies since July 2009 – goes from Seattle to Texas for four prospects.

July 10

1997: Pitcher **Jason McCommon** (1996-98) sees his streak of 24 scoreless innings come to a stunning halt as he allows first-inning homers to Bowie's **Augie Ojeda**, **David Dellucci** and **Chris Kirgan** before the Senators rally to win 5-4 on City Island.

2010: Padres pitcher **Chris Young** (2003) appears in his first All-Star Game, works the

fifth inning and allows a two-run, inside-the-park homer to Seattle's **Ichiro Suzuki** – the first inside-the-park homer in All Star Game history. Young also takes the loss as the National League falls 5-4 in San Francisco.

July 11

1865: Catcher **Pop Schriver** (1906-07), the oldest position player in Harrisburg history at age 42, born in Brooklyn, N.Y.

POP SCHRIVER

2002: The Expos trade pitchers **Justin Wayne** (2001-02), Carl Pavano, Graeme Lloyd and Donald Levinski, as well as infielder Mike Mordecai, to the Marlins for first baseman-outfielder **Cliff Floyd** (1993), infielder Wilton Guerrero, pitcher **Claudio Vargas** (2002-03) and $1.5 million. Vargas ends up helping the Senators reach the 2002 Eastern League finals.

2003: The Rangers trade pitcher **Ugueth Urbina** (1993-94) to the Marlins for first baseman Adrian Gonzalez, outfielder Will Smith and pitcher Ryan Snare.

UGUETH URBINA

July 12

1993: Center fielder **Rondell White** (1992-93, 1996) drives in three runs to lead the National League to a 12-7 victory in the Class AA All-Star Game in Memphis.

1994: One-time Pirates prospect **Moises Alou** (1989-90), now playing for the Expos, doubles home Hall of Famer Tony Gwynn with the winning run in the bottom of the 10th inning as the National League wins 9-8 in the All-Star Game at Pittsburgh's Three Rivers Stadium.

1999: A week after bolting Harrisburg to become an assistant coach at the University of Georgia, manager **Doug Sisson** (1999-2000) returns to the Senators and takes over a team that won four of seven games for interim manager **Rick Sweet** (1998-99).

July 13

1966: Pitcher **Rip Vowinkel** (1912) dies in Oswego, N.Y., at age 81.

2008: Pitcher **Shairon Martis** (2006, 2008, 2011) picks up the save for the World Team in a 3-0 shutout of Team USA in the Futures Game at Yankee Stadium.

2010: Bryce Harper (2011, 2013), playing for the College of Southern Nevada, receives the annual Golden Spikes Award as the nation's best collegiate player.

July 14

AL SCHACHT

1984: Pitcher **Al Schacht** (1915), the predecessor to **Max Patkin** as the "Clown Prince of Baseball," dies in Waterbury, Conn., at age 91.

1987: Twenty years before becoming the Senators' hitting coach, **Tim Raines** (2007) – then with Montreal – goes 3-for-3 with a two-run triple in the top of the 13th inning to lift the National League to a 2-0 victory at the All-Star Game in Oakland.

1995: After San Diego's players protest the team's pending promotion of would-be replacement player Ira Smith, Padres' management backs down and instead recalls first baseman **Archi Cianfrocco** (1991) from Class AAA. Smith, an outfielder, never reaches the majors, toiling another eight years in the minors before retiring.

1997: Infielder **Izzy Alcantara** (1995-97) begins a streak of homering in six straight games – an Eastern League record that falls one game shy of the minors' all-time record.

2010: In only the second Eastern League All-Star Game held on City Island, Altoona shortstop Chase d'Arnaud hits a grand slam in the seventh inning to clinch the Western Division's 10-3 victory over the East. A guest appearance by NASCAR driver Kevin Harvick helps spike the crowd to a then-City Island record of 8,078.

July 15

1908: Outfielder **Jake Powell** (1933) born in Silver Spring, Md.

1987: Second baseman **Jim Reboulet** (1987) extends his hitting streak to a franchise-record 32 straight games – a run that ends the next night when he is ejected in the third inning of a game at New Britain.

1997: Lee Smith, then baseball's all-time saves leader, announces his retirement from Montreal, leaving **Ugueth Urbina** (1993-94) to become the Expos' full-time closer.

2010: Cliff Lee (2002) becomes the first former Senators pitcher to start in the major leagues' All-Star Game, working two shutout innings for the American League at new Yankee Stadium. **Milton Bradley** (1999), Lee's teammate with Texas in 2010, also starts for the American League as its designated hitter.

2012: In a bit of gamesmanship in Miami, Marlins manager Ozzie Guillen complains about the amount of pine tar on the bat of Nationals rookie **Bryce Harper** (2011, 2013), prompting plate umpire Marty Foster to ask Harper to use a different bat on his next trip to the plate. That trip comes in the fourth inning, but not before Harper mockingly points his new bat toward the ever-combustible Guillen, who calls Harper's actions unprofessional.

2013: With his father Ron pitching to him, Nationals outfielder **Bryce Harper** (2011, 2013) finishes second to Oakland A's outfielder Yoenis Cespedes in the annual Home Run Derby on the eve of the All-Star Game at New York's Citi Field. Cespedes becomes the first right-handed hitter to win the Derby since former Senators right fielder **Vladimir Guerrero** (1996) in 2007. Twenty-four hours later, the 20-year-old Harper starts for the National League in center field and goes 0-2. Two other onetime Senators – Reds second baseman **Brandon Phillips** (2001-02) and Phillies pitcher **Cliff Lee** (2002) – also play for the NL with Phillips making his first All-Start start.

July 16

1926: **Andy Phillips** (1926) pitches the Senators' first no-hitter, beating Binghamton 9-0 in a seven-inning game.

1995: Outfielder **Tyrone Horne** (1992-95) is lifted for a pinch-hitter in the middle of an 11-2 loss at Norwich and told he has been traded – across the field to the other dugout as the Expos send him to the Yankees and their Class AA affiliate for infielder Dave Silvestri.

2000: Manager **Jim Tracy** (1993), then the Dodgers' bench coach, begins a four-game stint as their interim manager after Davey Johnson is hospitalized for an irregular heartbeat. After the season, Tracy replaces Johnson as the Dodgers' manager, a position Tracy holds for five seasons before spending another five-plus summers running the Pirates and Rockies.

JIM TRACY

July 17

1956: Cincinnati's **Brooks Lawrence** (1951), the Senators' first black pitcher, runs his record to 13-0 with a 4-3 victory over Brooklyn and Sandy Koufax at Crosley Field.

2001: Right fielder **Vladimir Guerrero** (1996) launches a 457-foot homer off Tim Wakefield as the Expos beat the Red Sox 11-7 at Olympic Stadium.

2010: Altoona scores 10 runs in the top of the ninth inning to beat the Senators 18-15 in one of the wildest games ever played on City Island.

July 18

1993: Outfielder **Melvin Nieves** (2005), then among Atlanta's top prospects, is traded by the Braves to San Diego for first baseman Fred McGriff.

1999: Shortstop **Orlando Cabrera** (1997) pops up to third baseman Scott Brosius for the final out as New York's David Cone completes the 16th perfect game in history, beating the Expos 6-0 at Yankee Stadium.

JOE BOLEY

July 19

1895: First baseman **Snake Henry** (1933) born in Waynesville, N.C.

1896: Shortstop **Joe Boley** (1917) born in Mahonoy City, Pa.

1966: Hitting coach **Tim Leiper** (1998) born in Whittier, Calif.

1973: Pitcher **Alex Pacheco** (1995-96) born in Caracas, Venz.

1994: The Eastern League announces plans to move its offices from Plainville, Conn., to City Island. The new digs, built by the city of Harrisburg for nearly $500,000, are used by the EL for less than two years. The EL offices move to Portland, Maine, after president John Levenda is fired in July 1996 and replaced by former Portland mayor Bill Troubh.

July 20

1944: Harrisburg Giants outfielder **Rap Dixon** (1922-27) dies in Detroit at age 41.

1988: Pitcher **Stephen Strasburg** (2010-11) born in San Diego, Calif.

1991: Starting with a 20-0 rout of the London Tigers on City Island, the Senators win 25 of the next 30 games on their way to an Eastern League-best record of 87-53.

1996: The Senators beat Bowie 3-2 before a then-record crowd of 6,438 on City Island.

July 21

1926: Just five days after teammate **Andy Phillips** (1926) no-hits Binghamton in a seven-inning game, **Marty Kinnere** (1925-26) beats Shamokin 2-0 in the Senators' first nine-inning no-hitter.

1956: The perfect 13-0 start for Reds pitcher **Brooks Lawrence** (1951) comes to an abrupt end at Crosley Field as the Pirates beat him 4-3 on Roberto Clemente's three-run homer in the top of the ninth inning.

1991: The Expos trade enigmatic pitcher Oil Can Boyd to Texas for three pitching prospects who greatly contribute to the Senators' successes from 1991-93 – **Jonathan Hurst** (1991), **Travis Buckley** (1992) and **Joey Eischen** (1993).

BROOKS LAWRENCE

1996: With his family visiting from Puerto Rico, third baseman **Jose Vidro** (1995-96, 2006) hits for the cycle in a 15-7 victory over Bowie on City Island. Four days later, Vidro drives in seven runs with a single, double and grand slam during an 11-0 rout at Trenton.

July 22

1973: Pitcher **Mike Thurman** (1996-97, 2000) born in Corvallis, Oregon.

July 23

1966: Pitcher **Len Picota** (1992) born in Panama City, Panama.

1996: Pitcher **Ed Wineapple** (1930) dies in Delray Beach, Fla., at age 90.

1998: The Expos call up pitcher **Jeremy Powell** (1998) to start against the Cubs at Wrigley Field, where Powell allows only three hits in six innings of a 2-1 loss. After the game, the Expos return Powell to Harrisburg.

July 24

1968: First baseman **Rob Lukachyk** (1996-97) born in Jersey City, N.J.

1973: Infielder **Jhonny Carvajal** (1996-98, 2000) born in Anzoategui, Venz.

1994: Center fielder **Rondell White** (1992-93, 1996) drives in all seven runs for the Expos in a 7-4 victory over the Dodgers in Montreal.

2008: Manager **John Stearns** (2006, 2008-09) picks up his 500th career victory as the Senators win 8-7 at Bowie.

July 25

1971: Catcher **Chief Meyers** (1906) dies in San Bernardino, Calif., at age 90.

1973: Pitcher **Guillermo Mota** (1998) born in San Pedro de Macoris, D.R.

1976: Pitcher **Javier Vazquez** (1997) born in Ponce, P.R.

1988: Player-manager and onetime Yankees prospect **Glenn Killinger** (1924, 1927-28) dies in Newark, Del., at age 89.

1995: Right fielder **Kevin Northrup** (1994-95), the Eastern League's top hitter in 1994, is told by Senators manager **Pat Kelly** (1995-96) during batting practice in Reading that he is being traded by the Expos to the A's for pitcher Dave Leiper, the brother of future Senators hitting coach **Tim Leiper** (1998).

2002: The Dodgers trade infielder **Hiram Bocachica** (1997-98) to the Tigers for pitchers Tom Farmer and Jason Frasor.

GLENN KILLINGER

July 26

1993: The Rockies trade pitchers **Doug Bochtler** (1992) and Andy Ashby, and catcher Brad Ausmus, to the Padres for pitchers Bruce Hurst and Greg Harris.

2000: Pitcher **Donnie Bridges** (2000-02, 2004-05) allows one hit through six innings and hits a solo homer in the third inning for the Senators' only run in a 1-0 victory at Portland.

2007: Pitcher **John Lannan** (2007, 2010) sees his major league debut with the Nationals unexpectedly end in the bottom of the fifth inning as quick-tempered plate umpire Hunter Wendelstedt ejects the left-hander after he hits Philadelphia's Chase Utley and Ryan Howard – both left-handed batters – on consecutive pitches in a one-run game.

2011: The Nationals trade outfielder-first baseman **Bill Rhinehart** (2008-11) and pitcher Chris Manno to Cincinnati for well-traveled outfielder Jonny Gomes.

July 27

1967: Pitcher **Linc Mikkelsen** (1995) born in Montague, Mich.

1982: Catcher **Devin Ivany** (2007-08, 2010-12) born in Plantation, Fla.

1988: Future pitching coach **Tommy John** (2002), playing with the Yankees, accomplishes an ignominious feat that no other pitcher has done in 120 years of pro baseball as he commits three errors on one play in New York's 16-3 beating of Milwaukee at Yankee Stadium. The gaffes take place with one out in the fourth inning as John first mishandles

MATT LeCROY

Jeffrey Leonard's grounder for error No. 1, which he follows up with two more throwing errors that allow two runs – including one by Leonard – to score.

1953: The Hall of Fame inducts pitcher **Chief Bender** (1902) in a class that includes pitcher Dizzy Dean and outfielder Al Simmons.

1996: Future manager **Matt LeCroy** (2012-13) is one of seven Americans to homer in Team USA's 15-5 victory over Japan during the Olympics in Atlanta.

1998: Outfielder **Tyrone Horne** (1992-95), playing for Class AA Arkansas, hits for the rarest of cycles with a solo homer, two-run homer, three-run homer and grand slam in a 13-4 Texas League victory over San Antonio.

2010: When rookie **Stephen Strasburg** (2010-11) – a week past his 22nd birthday – cannot make his scheduled start against Atlanta because of shoulder tightness he is replaced at the last moment by 39-year-old **Miguel Batista** (1993-94), who throws five shutout innings in the Nationals' 3-0 home win.

2013: The Senators take an early 2-0 lead but cannot hold off the Portland Sea Dogs before falling 5-2 in the eighth annual "Futures at Fenway" game in Boston.

July 28

1936: **Bill "Bullfrog" Dietrich** (1931), already waived twice that season by the A's and Washington Senators, makes his first start with the White Sox – collecting four hits, pitching a complete game and beating his old Philadelphia teammates 19-6 at Comiskey Park.

July 29

1880: Catcher **Chief Meyers** (1906) born in Riverside, Calif.

1938: Yankees outfielder **Jake Powell** (1933) punctuates a postgame radio interview after New York's 4-3 victory over the White Sox in Chicago with racial epithets, prompting commissioner Kennesaw Landis to suspend Powell for 10 days.

1963: Outfielder **Tommy Gregg** (1987) born in Boone, N.C.

1968: Outfielder **Rob Katzaroff** (1991) born in Long Beach, Calif.

2000: Light-hitting shortstop **Josh Reding** (2000-02) leads off the bottom of the ninth with a homer to lift the Senators over New Haven 11-10.

2009: In a move that helps them reach the World Series, the Phillies acquire pitcher **Cliff Lee** (2002) and outfielder Ben Francisco from Cleveland for four minor leaguers.

July 30

1995: One hundred years after making his pro debut on City Island, pitcher **Vic Willis** (1895) is inducted into the Hall of Fame, along with Mike Schmidt, Richie Ashburn, Leon Day and William Hulbert.

2002: After trading for him a few weeks earlier, the Expos send first baseman-outfielder **Cliff Floyd** (1993) to Boston for pitchers **Seung Song** (2002-03) and Sun Woo Kim.

2004: The Dodgers trade pitcher **Guillermo Mota** (1998), catcher Paul LoDuca and outfielder Juan Encarnacion to the Marlins for pitchers Brad Penny and Bill Murphy, and first baseman Hee Seop Choi.

2006: Long-ago Harrisburg infielders **Frank Grant** (1890) and **Ben Taylor** (1925) are among the 17 Negro Leaguers and their predecessors inducted into Hall of Fame. Narrowly missing induction are onetime Harrisburg outfielders **Spottswood Poles** (1906-08), **Rap Dixon** (1922-27) and **Fats Jenkins** (1923-27), as well as former Giants infielder **John Beckwith** (1926-27).

2011: For the third time in his career, shortstop **Orlando Cabrera** (1997) switches teams at the trading deadline, this time moving from the Indians to the Giants for outfielder Thomas Neal.

ORLANDO CABRERA

2011: Shortstop **Zach Walters** (2012) is acquired by the Nationals from Arizona for pitcher **Jason Marquis** (2010).

July 31

1961: Outfielder **Bud Weiser** (1925) dies in Shamokin, Pa., at age 70.

1993: The Pirates trade pitcher **Stan Belinda** (1989) to the Royals for pitchers Jon Lieber and Dan Miceli.

1996: The Dodgers send pitchers **Joey Eischen** (1993) and John Cummings to Detroit for outfielder Chad Curtis.

2000: The Expos deal outfielder **Rondell White** (1992-93, 1996) to the Cubs for pitcher Scott Downs.

2001: John Stephens strikes out 13 in no-hitting the Senators 2-0 at Bowie.

2001: The Expos trade closer **Ugueth Urbina** (1993-94) to Boston for pitchers **Rich Rundles** (2004-05) and Tomo Ohka, and also send center fielder **Milton Bradley** (1999) to Cleveland for pitcher **Zach Day** (2005).

2004: Shortstop **Orlando Cabrera** (1997) is part of a three-shortstop trade with Cabrera going from Montreal to Boston, which sends Nomar Garciaparra to the Cubs, who ship shortstop Alex Gonzalez to the Expos.

2007: The Senators reach the 5-million mark in attendance on City Island for the modern era during a 10-1 victory over New Hampshire.

2009: The A's trade shortstop **Orlando Cabrera** (1997) to the Twins for minor league infielder Tyler Ladendorf.

2010: Cleveland deals pitcher **Jake Westbrook** (1999) to St. Louis in a three-team, four-player trade that sends Cardinals outfielder Ryan Ludwick to San Diego.

August 1

1865: Hall of Fame infielder **Frank Grant** (1890) born in Pittsfield, Mass.

1993: First baseman-outfielder **Cliff Floyd** (1993) is promoted from Harrisburg to Class AAA Ottawa, leaving behind an MVP season for the Senators in which he bats .329 in 101 games with modern-franchise records for homers with 26 and RBIs at 101.

1995: Would-be replacement player **Antonio Grissom** (1995) becomes the first player

in the Senators' modern era to end a game with a grand slam as his walk-off shot off Brett Cederblad leads to an 8-4 victory over Trenton on City Island.

2007: Reds second baseman **Brandon Phillips** (2001-02) steals second and third on the same play as he takes advantage of the Nationals' exaggerated shift against pull-happy **Adam Dunn** with third baseman **Ryan Zimmerman** (2005) playing on the right-field side of second base. The steals off pitcher **John Lannan** (2007, 2010) and catcher **Brian Schneider** (1999) come in the top of the fourth inning of Washington's 7-2 victory at Nationals Park.

2011: Outfielder **Joe Caffie** (1951), the Senators' first black position player, dies in Warren, Ohio at age 80.

BRANDON PHILLIPS

August 2

1993: Pirates second baseman **Carlos Garcia** (1989-90) homers twice – his only career multi-homer game – in a 12-10 loss to the Cubs at Wrigley Field.

August 3

1947: Hall of Fame pitcher **Vic Willis** (1895) dies in Elkton, Md., at age 71.

1972: Pitcher **Ben Fleetham** (1994, 1996-97) born in Minneapolis, Minn.

1973: Pitcher **Blake Stein** (2003) born in McComb, Miss.

1998: Outfielder **Peter Bergeron** (1998-99) and first baseman **Jon Tucker** (1998-99), integral members of the 1998 and '99 championship teams, arrive on City Island from the Dodgers' Class AA affiliate in San Antonio after being acquired by the Expos in the July 31 trade that sends and one-time All-Stars **Mark Grudzielanek** (1994) and **Carlos Perez** (1994), as well as infielder **Hiram Bocachica** (1997-98), to the Dodgers.

HIRAM BOCACHICA

August 4

2011: Phillies pitcher **Cliff Lee** (2002) beats San Francisco 3-0 for the fifth of his eventual major league high six shutouts.

August 5

1955: After 274 straight games, **Nellie Fox** – the pride of St. Thomas, Pa. – is told by White Sox manager Marty Marion to take the day off. The Hall of Fame second baseman starts another streak the next day, playing in another 798 straight games before his next rest.

August 6

1966: Pitcher **Stan Belinda** (1989) born in Huntingdon, Pa.

1989: Pirates first baseman **Jeff King** (1987-88) goes hitless in his first seven trips to the plate before starting the bottom of the 18th inning with a homer to deep left field off the Cubs' Scott Sanderson for a 5-4 victory at Three Rivers Stadium in Pittsburgh.

1998: Batting cleanup for the first time in his career, infielder **Geoff Blum** (1996, 1998) hits for the ultra-rare natural cycle – a single, followed in order by double, triple

GEOFF BLUM

and homer – in a 3-2 victory over New Haven on City Island. After the game, Blum's bat is sent to the Hall of Fame before being returned to Harrisburg and sold at a charity auction.

2009: Minor League Baseball suspends infielder **Ofilio Castro** (2007-10) and outfielder **Edgardo Baez** (2008-10) each 50 games for using amphetamines.

August 7

CHRIS HANEY

1984: Outfielder **Jimmy Van Ostrand** (2012-13) born in Vancouver, B.C.

1999: Cleveland's **Chris Haney** (1991) becomes the first pitcher to allow an opponent's 3,000th hit to come on a home run as he serves one up to Tampa Bay's Wade Boggs in the sixth inning of the Indians' 15-10 victory at Tropicana Field.

2010: Three weeks after scoring 10 runs in the top of the ninth to beat the Senators 18-15 on City Island, Altoona again scores 10 in the top of the ninth against the Senators in an 18-6 victory.

August 8

1963: Pitcher **Brett Gideon** (1987-88) born in Ozona, Tex.

1987: The Senators travel to Pittsburgh for a home game against Albany-Colonie and play into the eighth inning before the game is suspended with the score tied at 3. The game resumes the next day on City Island, where the Yankees win 7-3 in 12 innings.

1990: The Pirates trade outfielders **Moises Alou** (1989-90) and Willie Greene, and pitcher **Scott Ruskin** (1989), to the Expos for pitcher Zane Smith.

1995: Third baseman **Jeff King** (1987-88) homers twice off Sergio Valdez and Terry Mulholland during the Pirates' nine-run second inning in a 9-5 victory at San Francisco, becoming the first Pirate to homer twice in an inning since outfielder Jake Stenzel in 1894.

August 9

2002: Right fielder **Vladimir Guerrero** (1996) hits his 200th career homer in the majors, a solo shot to left-center off Milwaukee's Mike DeJean to start the ninth inning of the Expos' 11-4 victory at Miller Park.

2005: Outfielder **Brandon Watson** (2002-03, 2005) doubles and homers in his first three at-bats in the majors as the Nationals win 6-5 at Houston.

August 10

1905: Pitcher **Ed Wineapple** (1930) born in Boston, Mass.

2003: In his Class AA debut, **Shawn Hill** (2003-04, 2006) becomes the first pitcher in the Senators' modern era to hit a grand slam as his drive to left field – also coming in his

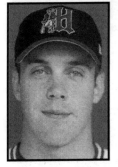

first professional at-bat – beats Altoona 4-1 at Blair County Ballpark.

2007: Outfielder **Steve Mortimer** (2007) joins **Matt Stairs** (1991), **Jose Vidro** (1996) and **Geoff Blum** (1998) as the only Senators to hit for the cycle in the team's modern era when he goes 4-for-4 in an 8-3 victory at Portland.

2010: Pitcher **Orlando "El Duque" Hernandez** (2010), out of the majors since 2007, joins the Senators. At 44, he is the oldest player in Harrisburg history.

2011: Outfielder **Bryce Harper** (2011, 2013) who at 18 is Harrisburg' youngest player since second baseman **Bob Keller** in

SHAWN HILL

1935, earns his first ejection in Class AA when he spikes his helmet after being called out on strikes by plate umpire Max Guyll for the last out of the seventh inning. Replays show the pitch from Richmond's Eric Surkamp is outside. Videos of Harper's meltdown quickly go viral on the Internet.

August 11

1935: Two former Harrisburg Giants – Hall of Fame player-manager **Oscar Charleston** (1924-27) and outfielder **Fats Jenkins** (1924-27) – are among the starters in the Negro Leagues' East-West Game at Chicago's Comiskey Park.

1958: Pitcher **Dorn Taylor** (1987) born in Abington, Pa.

1979: Outfielder **Jorge Padilla** (2008) born in Rio Piedras, P.R.

1987: Pitcher **Drew Storen** (2009-10, 2012) born in Indianapolis.

FATS JENKINS

2007: The Senators have a major league experience with a disappointing result as they travel to Boston's Fenway Park for a day game, only to watch Portland rally four times to beat them 12-11 as part of the Red Sox's second annual Futures at Fenway series before a crowd of 34,746.

August 12

1968: Outfielder **Tony Longmire** (1988-90) born in Vallejo, Calif.

1985: Catcher **Jhonatan Solano** (2009-10, 2012) born in Barranquilla, Colombia.

1999: Third baseman **Andy Tracy** (1998-99) homers in a 10-4 victory at Binghamton, giving him 28 and breaking the modern franchise single-season record set just two years earlier by **Izzy Alcantara** (1995-97). Tracy finishes the season with 37 homers and 128 RBIs, one RBI shy of matching the all-time franchise record set by outfielder **Joe Munson** (1925).

2011: Teenage outfielder **Bryce Harper** (2011, 2013) launches a two-run homer over the center-field batter's eye in the bottom of the ninth to beat Reading 3-2. The 18-year-old Harper tweaks his right hamstring less than a week later and misses the rest of the season.

ANDY TRACY

August 13

1961: Second baseman **Jim Reboulet** (1987) born in Dayton, Ohio.

1964: Catcher **Tom Prince** (1987) born in Kankakee, Ill.

1991: The night after he uncorks two wild pitches in a 5-4 loss at Reading, reliever **William Brennan** (1991) unloads a modern franchise-record four wild pitches in one inning – the seventh – but they represent no problem in the Senators' 14-3 victory over the Reading Phillies at Municipal Stadium.

1998: The Senators score a modern franchise-record 11 runs in one inning – the sixth – during an 11-6 victory at Trenton.

August 14

1964: Infielder **Tommy Shields** (1988-89) born in Fairfax, Va.

2008: Less than a month after celebrating his 20th birthday, **Stephen Strasburg** (2010-11) brings his enormous talent to the international stage, striking out 11 over seven innings in a 7-0 victory over the Netherlands at the Olympics in Beijing. The losing pitcher is **Shairon Martis** (2006, 2008, 2011).

August 15

1864: Utility player **Doggie Miller** (1893) born in Brooklyn, N.Y.

1963: Hitting coach **Eric Fox** (2001, 2012-13) born in Lemoore, Calif.

1981: Pitcher **Oliver Perez** (2011) born in Culiacan, Mexico.

2008: Pitcher **Darrin Winston** (1993-94) dies in Freehold, N.J., at age 42.

August 16

1990: The Pirates inform the Senators they will not renew their player-development contract after the season, ending the teams' four-year affiliation.

2010: Pitcher **Jonathan Albaladejo** (2007) finishes Scranton/Wilkes-Barre's 7-4 victory at Toledo with his 39th save, breaking the Class AAA International League record set by Matt Whiteside in 2004. Albaladejo finishes the season with 43 saves.

2010: After navigating their way through the usual gamesmanship negotiations with uber-agent Scott Boras, the Nationals wait until the final minutes before the signing deadline to get the autograph of the draft's first overall pick, 17-year-old outfielder **Bryce Harper** (2011, 2013), on a five-year contract worth $9.9 million.

August 17

1966: Right fielder **Tony Barron** (1995-96) born in Portland, Ore.

1976: Catcher **Yohanny Valera** (2000) born in Santo Domingo, D.R.

1980: Pitcher **Mike O'Connor** (2007, 2009) born in Dallas, Tex.

1999: Among the high school juniors participating in the first Mid-Atlantic Scouts Association Invitational Showcase on City Island is David Wright, a third baseman from Chesapeake, Va., who eventually becomes a perennial All-Star with the Mets.

2006: Trenton's Tyler Clippard no-hits the Senators 3-0 on City Island.

2009: With only 77 seconds remaining before the midnight signing deadline, the Nationals agree to a deal with top overall draft pick **Stephen Strasburg** (2010-11) – another Scott Boras client – that pays the pitcher a first-contract record of $15.1 million over four years.

August 18

1974: Pitcher **Jayson Durocher** (1998-99) born in Hartford, Conn.

1974: Outfielder **Chris Stowers** (1997-98) born in St. Louis, Mo.

2004: Shortstop **Josh Labandeira** (2003-05) and second baseman **Alejandro Machado** (2004) combine for 19 chances and three double plays in a 6-4 loss to Altoona on City Island.

August 19

1902: Player-manager **Kip Selbach** (1907-08, 1910-11), playing with the Baltimore Orioles, becomes the first American League outfielder in the 20th century to commit five errors in one game, including three in one inning, in an 11-4 loss to the St. Louis Browns.

1969: Outfielder **Tyrone Woods** (1992-94) born in Dade City, Fla.

August 20

1973: Pitcher **Jose Paniagua** (1995-96) born in San Jose de Ocoa, D.R.

1978: Pitcher **T.J. Tucker** (1999-2001) born in Clearwater, Fla.

1978: Pitcher **Chris Schroder** (2003-06) born in Okarche, Okla.

2011: The Senators draw their 6 millionth fan since their return to City Island in 1987.

August 21

1938: Former Harrisburg Giants infielder **Rev Cannady** (1925-27) starts at second base for the East in a 5-4 loss in the Negro Leagues' East-West game at Comiskey Park. One-time Giants teammate and Hall of Famer **Oscar Charleston** (1924-27) manages the East.

1951: Manager **John Stearns** (2006, 2008-09) born in Denver, Colo.

1971: Pitcher **Lou Pote** (1995-96) born in Evergreen Park, Ill.

2003: A solo homer by **Vladimir Guerrero** (1996) off Odalis Perez in the third inning of the Expos' 2-1 loss at Dodger Stadium gives him 226 in his career to break the Expos' franchise record held by Hall of Famer Andre Dawson.

2010: Pitcher **Willie Fordham** (1952) dies in Camp Hill, Pa., at age 83.

2010: Utility player **Matt Stairs** (1991), playing for San Diego, launches a record-setting 21st homer as a pinch-hitter with a two-run shot to right field off Milwaukee's Kameron Loe in the eighth inning of the Padres' 6-5 loss at Miller Park.

MATT STAIRS

August 22

1927: Ollie Hanson (1927) pitches the Senators' third no-hitter, beating Binghamton 4-0.

1989: Indians shortstop **Felix Fermin** (1987) ties a major league record with four sacrifice bunts in a 3-2 victory over Seattle in 10 innings. Fermin is the first to accomplish the feat since Cleveland's Ray Chapman in 1919.

1991: Well, somebody had to do it and that somebody is **Randy Tomlin** (1989-90) as the Pirates' left-hander becomes the first to hit John Kruk with a pitch after the Phillies' All-Star first baseman goes his first 2,681 at-bats in the majors without being plunked.

1996: Right fielder **Vladimir Guerrero** (1996) is named the Eastern League's MVP, joining **Wes Chamberlain** (1989), **Matt Stairs** (1991), **Cliff Floyd** (1993) and **Mark Grudzielanek** (1994) as Senators to win the award since 1989.

1999: Pitcher **Jake Westbrook** (1999) allows a first-inning infield single to Brendan Kingman and nothing else in one-hitting over New Haven 2-0 on City Island.

2003: Manager **Dave Machemer** (2003-04) earns his 1,000th career victory in the Senators' 10-8 win over Akron on City Island.

2010: Manager **Mike Quade** (1991-92) becomes the Cubs' interim manager after Lou Piniella resigns. Quade keeps the job through 2011.

August 23

1936: Harrisburg Giants Hall of Famer **Oscar Charleston** (1924-27) manages the East to a 10-2 victory in the Negro Leagues' East-West game in Chicago.

1991: Utility player **Matt Stairs** (1991) becomes the first player in the Senators' modern era to hit for the cycle during a 7-4 loss to New Britain on City Island.

1994: Shortstop **Mark Grudzielanek** (1994) is named the Eastern League's MVP while **Dave Jauss** (1994) is voted manager of the year.

August 24

1971: Pitcher **Everett Stull** (1995-96) born in Fort Riley, Kan.

August 25

1931: **Andy Rush** (1931-32) no-hits Scranton 6-0 in a seven-inning game.

1993: The Eastern League names first baseman-outfielder **Cliff Floyd** (1993) its MVP, making Floyd the third Senator to win the honor after right fielder **Wes Chamberlain** (1989) and utility player **Matt Stairs** (1991). The EL also names **Joey Eischen** (1993) its pitcher of the year and **Jim Tracy** (1993) as the manager of the year.

1995: The Senators draw their 2 millionth fan in modern-franchise history for a 7-2 loss to Reading on City Island.

2004: Outfielder **Jeremy Ware** (1999-2004) hits a solo homer but that is not nearly enough as Canada falls to Japan 11-2 in the bronze medal game at Olympics in Athens, Greece. The Canadian team includes eight past, present and future Senators with coaches **Denis Boucher** (1996) and **Tim Leiper** (1998); and pitchers **Mike Johnson** (1998), **Shawn Hill** (2003-04, 2006) and **John Ogiltree** (2005), as well as Ware, infielder **Simon Pond** (1998) and hitting coach **Rob Ducey** (2004), who is one of Canada's designated hitters.

August 26

1909: Outfielder **Gene Moore** (1932) born in Lancaster, Tex.

1934: Harrisburg Giants Hall of Famer **Oscar Charleston** (1924-27) and outfielder **Rap Dixon** (1922-27) play for the East in a 1-0 victory in the East-West game at Comiskey Park.

1975: Pitcher **Troy Mattes** (1999-2000, 2003) born in Champaign, Ill.

2010: In his first start of the season for Washington after recovering from Tommy John surgery, **Jordan Zimmermann** (2008, 2010) gives up Albert Pujols' 400th career homer in an 11-10 victory over St. Louis in 13 innings at Nationals Park.

2011: Shairon Martis (2006, 2008, 2011) throws a seven-inning, no-hitter as the Senators win 3-0 in the first game of a doubleheader at New Hampshire.

August 27

1939: In the second East-West game of the Negro League season, former Harrisburg Giant **Oscar Charleston** (1924-27) manages the East in a 10-2 loss at Yankee Stadium.

1955: Manager **Pat Kelly** (1995-96) born in Santa Maria, Calif.

1967: Pitcher **Willie Smith** (1989) born in Savannah, Ga.

1974: Infielder **Jose Vidro** (1995-96, 2006) born in Mayaguez, P.R.

1995: Expos pitcher **Kirk Rueter** (1993) allows only a third-inning single to Kirk Manwaring as he beats San Francisco 1-0 on a one-hitter in Montreal.

1999: Expos right fielder **Vladimir Guerrero** (1996) grounds out, walks and fouls out to end his 31-game hitting streak in a 4-1 loss to the Reds at Olympic Stadium. He is waiting on-deck when **Jose Vidro** (1995-96, 2006) flies out to end the game.

August 28

1950: Hall of Famer Willie Mays homers against the Senators on City Island – one of only four home runs Trenton's 19-year-old center fielder hits that summer in the Class B Interstate League.

1971: Third baseman **Shane Andrews** (1993) born in Dallas, Tex.

WILLIE MAYS

August 29

1919: Shortstop **Billy Cox** (1940-41) born in Newport, Pa.

1992: The Expos trade pitchers **Bill Sampen** (1988-89) and **Chris Haney** (1991) to Kansas City for pitcher **Archie Corbin** (1993) and third baseman Sean Berry.

1998: A record crowd on City Island of 6,737 sees the Senators lose 7-1 to Bowie.

2008: With a full month remaining in the American League season, **Cliff Floyd** (1993) drives in five runs as the Tampa Bay Rays beat the Orioles 14-3 at home to clinch the once beleaguered franchise's first winning record on its way to the World Series.

2010: Onetime World Series hero **Orlando "El Duque" Hernandez** (2010), then 44 and trying to revive a career stalled since 2007, leaves the Senators before they embark on a season-ending road trip to New Hampshire and Binghamton.

2012: Both the talent and temper of outfielder **Bryce Harper** (2011, 2013) are on full display in Miami as the 19-year-old rookie homers twice before being ejected in the ninth inning for slamming his helmet in frustration after hitting into a double play during the Nationals' 8-4 victory over the Marlins. The ejection is Harper's first in the majors.

August 30

1978: Pitcher **Cliff Lee** (2002) born in Benton, Ark.

2000: Donnie Bridges (2000-02, 2004-05) beats Erie 2-0 to become the first Senators pitcher in their modern era to throw four shutouts in one season.

DONNIE BRIDGES

August 31

2007: Outfielder **Roger Bernadina** (2007-08) becomes the first player in the Senators' modern era to hit two grand slams in a season with a bases-loaded drive to deep right field off Reading's Carlos Carrasco in the second inning of an 8-6 victory on City Island.

2011: The Senators beat Portland 2-1 on City Island to clinch a playoff berth for the second straight season. The night, though, ends poorly for outfielder **Archie Gilbert** (2011), the Senators' top hitter with a .313 batting average, as he is charged with DUI after allegedly turning a construction zone along Route 581 into his personal race course and narrowly avoiding striking an overnight work crew. The Nationals suspend Gilbert for the upcoming playoffs, where the Senators are swept in three games by Richmond.

September 1

1988: A year after leading the Eastern League with a .371 batting average, outfielder **Tommy Gregg** (1987) is sent by the Pirates to the Braves for third baseman Ken Oberkfell.

1993: Thanks to a crowd of 4,551 for their final regular-season home game, the Senators reach 250,000 in attendance for the first time in team history.

1994: Solo homers by **Mark Grudzielanek** (1994), **Tyrone Horne** (1992-95) and **Mike Hardge** (1993-94) lift the Senators over Bowie 3-2 on City Island, despite 16 strikeouts by Baysox right-hander Jimmy Haynes. The strikeouts are the most by an opposing pitcher against the Senators since their return in 1987. Reading's Jesse Biddle ties Haynes' mark in 2013 during the Fightin Phils' 3-2 victory on the island.

1997: After hitting nine home runs in August, **Izzy Alcantara** (1995-97) homers in a 6-5 victory at Reading in the Senators' final game, giving him 27 for the season to break the modern-franchise record he had shared with **Cliff Floyd** (1993) and **Glenn Murray** (1993).

2003: Outfielder **Brandon Watson** (2002-03, 2005) goes 1-for-5 in the season finale – a 6-3 victory at Norwich – to finish with 180 hits, the most in the Senators' modern era.

2011: With a City Island-record crowd of 8,637 looking on, the Senators beat Portland 10-0 to earn their first division title since 1997. The title seems secondary to the injury re-hab starts made by pitcher **Stephen Strasburg** (2010-11) and longtime major league catch-er **Ivan Rodriguez** (2011), as well as the return of a popular attraction called "Cowboy Monkeys." Think of monkeys riding atop dogs while herding goats and you get the idea.

September 2

1901: Harrisburg Giants outfielder **Rap Dixon** (1922-27) born in Kingston, Ga.

1932: **Lew Krausse** (1933-35) of the A's beats the Red Sox 15-0 at Shibe Park in the last major league game for the 20-year-old pitcher. Five days later, Krausse injures his arm in an exhibition game against Class D Stroudsburg and ends up in Harrisburg within a year.

1990: The Senators win 10-1 at London in their final game as the Pirates' AA affiliate.

2001: Needing nine strikeouts to match the franchise record of 160 set by **Rich Sauveur** (1987), **Ron Chiavacci** (2001-03) strikes out 10 in seven innings of a 5-4, 10-inning victory over Erie on City Island.

September 3

1924: Hilldale pitcher Nip Walters throws the first no-hitter in the history of the Eastern Colored League, beating the Harrisburg Giants 2-0 on City Island.

1933: A year removed from his last game in the majors, **Lew Krausse** (1933-35) no-hits York 3-0 in a nine-inning game.

1991: After hitting .383 over the season's final month, utility player **Matt Stairs** (1991) is named the Eastern League's MVP. **Mike Quade** (1991-92) is picked as the top manager.

2004: Shortstop **Josh Labandeira** (2003-05) homers to start a 7-6 win at Akron, mark-ing the sixth time – a modern-franchise record – he homers to lead off a game.

2012: In the season finale, players from the Senators and Bowie – just for kicks – share the same bat for two-plus innings before the Baysox's Robbie Widlansky accidentally breaks the lumber on a single in the top of the third of Harrisburg's 7-2 loss on City Island.

September 4

1976: Outfielder **Ron Calloway** (2001-02) born in San Jose, Calif.

1991: Infielder **Tommy Shields** (1988-89) and Rochester teammate Shane Turner each play all nine positions in an 8-0 victory over Syracuse in the final game of Class AAA International League season.

September 5

TOMMY SHIELDS

1977: Pitcher **Ron Chiavacci** (2001-03) born in Scranton, Pa.

1978: Outfielder **Matt Watson** (2002) born in Lancaster, Pa.

1993: Center fielder **Glenn Murray** (1993) homers in the second inning of a 3-0 victory at Binghamton, giving him 26 for the season and tying him with teammate **Cliff Floyd** (1993) for the Eastern League lead.

2000: The Senators beat Akron 8-1 at Canal Park in a special play-in game for the right to face Reading in the Eastern League's Southern Division finals, which Reading wins in a three-game sweep of the four-time defending EL champions.

2007: Second baseman **Brandon Phillips** (2001-02) jumpstarts the Reds' 7-0 victory over the Mets in Cincinnati with a two-run homer in the first inning off John Maine, giving him 28 – on his way to 30 – for the summer and breaking the franchise's single-season record for home runs by a second baseman set in 1976 by Hall of Famer Joe Morgan.

September 6

1964: Pitcher **Mike York** (1988-89) born in Oak Park, Ill.

1978: Outfielder **Alex Escobar** (2006-07) born in Valencia, Venz.

1988: Pitcher **Lew Krausse** (1933-35) dies in Sarasota, Fla., at age 76.

1993: Pitcher **Denis Boucher** (1996) and catcher **Joe Siddall** (1991-92) give the Expos the second all-Canadian battery in history in a 4-3 win over the Rockies at Olympic Stadium.

JOE SIDDALL

The first such pairing came 110 years earlier with Tip O'Neill and John Humphries for the New York Metropolitans.

2000: A year after stunning Norwich with a title-winning, walk-off grand slam by **Milton Bradley** (1999), the Senators are equally flummoxed as pinch-hitter Carmine Cappuccio lifts an opposite-field, game-ending slam off **Rodney Stevenson** (1997-2000) to cap a six-run rally in the ninth inning as Reading stuns Harrisburg 10-9 in Game 1 of the Southern Division finals at Municipal Stadium. Reading sweeps the series in three games.

2004: The Senators drop their season finale 12-4 at Akron, ending the season at 52-90 for their worst finish since returning to City Island in 1987.

2011: A year after undergoing Tommy John surgery and five days after making a final rehab start on City Island, **Stephen Strasburg** (2010-11) pitches five shutout innings for Washington in a no-decision against the Dodgers at Nationals Park.

September 7

1952: Manager **Rick Sweet** (1998-99) born in Longview, Wash.

1968: Outfielder **Julio Peguero** (1989-90) born in San Isidro, D.R.

1993: Pitcher **Joe Ausanio** (1990, 1993) turns in the finest relief performance in the Senators' modern era, striking out seven in the final 4 1/3 innings of a 7-6, 12-inning victory over the Albany-Colonie Yankees in Game 2 of the Eastern League semifinals. The effort helps prompt the New York Yankees to select Ausanio two months later in the Rule V draft.

1997: Right-hander **Javier Vazquez** (1997) beats Portland 9-1 at Hadlock Field in the first game of the best-of-5 EL finals. The start is Vazquez's last with the Senators, capping a short Class AA stay in which the future All-Star goes 6-0 with two no-decisions.

JOE AUSANIO

1997: A double to left-center by **Mark Grudzielanek** (1994) off Ryan Karp in the eighth inning of the Expos' 2-1 loss to the Phillies in Montreal is his 49th to break the single-season record for shortstops set in 1932 by Philadelphia's Dick Bartell. Grudzielanek ends the season with 54 doubles, a record Boston's Nomar Garciaparra breaks in 2002 with 56.

2008: San Diego's **Chris Young** (2003) comes within four outs of pitching a perfect game before Milwaukee's Gabe Kapler homers with two outs in the bottom of the eighth inning in a game Young wins 10-1 at Miller Park.

September 8

1987: Catcher **Tom Prince** (1987), left fielder **Tommy Gregg** (1987) and pitcher **Rich Sauveur** (1987) are named to the Eastern League's postseason all-star team, while **Dave Trembley** (1987-89) is named the EL's manager of the year.

2000: Reading completes a three-game sweep of the Senators on City Island in the first round of the playoffs, depriving Harrisburg of a chance to build on its Eastern League-record four straight championships.

2002: The Senators win 5-1 in Akron to clinch the first round of the EL playoffs and move into the finals for the eighth time in 12 seasons as Montreal's Class AA affiliate.

2011: After winning an Eastern League-high 80 games, the Senators are forced to open the playoffs on the road as flooding from Tropical Storm Lee leaves City Island unplayable.

2012: The Nationals follow through on their preseason plan to shut down pitcher **Stephan Strasburg** (2010-11) as he nears 160 innings. Strasburg, barely a year removed from completing his injury rehab for 2010 Tommy John surgery, finishes the season at 15-6 with 197 strikeouts in 159 1/3 innings. Many pundits believe shutting down Strasburg costs the National League East champions a chance to reach World Series.

September 9

1997: Playoff MVP **Trey Moore** (1997) strikes out 11 in 7 2/3 innings as the Senators beat Portland 2-1 in Game 3 of the Eastern League finals to give Harrisburg a 2-1 lead in a best-of-5 series they will win in four games.

September 10

1933: Now playing for different teams, the Harrisburg Giants' once-vaunted outfield of Hall of Famer **Oscar Charleston** (1924-27), **Fats Jenkins** (1923-27) and **Rap Dixon** (1922-27) is reunited on the East team in the Negro Leagues' first East-West Game at Chicago's Comiskey Park. Charleston, then with the famed Pittsburgh Crawfords, is the game's leading vote getter with 43,793 in fan balloting conducted by the country's major black newspapers. He starts at first base as the East falls to the West 11-7.

1987: A two-out homer in the bottom of the ninth by **Tom Prince** (1987) off Todd Frohwirth ties the score at 2 before the Senators beat Reading 3-2 in 13 innings of the fifth and deciding game of the Eastern League semifinals.

1991: The Senators fall to Albany-Colonie 4-1 in the third and final game of the Eastern League finals.

1993: **Tyrone Woods** (1992-94) launches a two-run homer at Heritage Park to fuel an 8-4 victory over Albany-Colonie in the fourth and deciding game of the EL semis.

TYRONE WOODS

September 11

1996: The Senators win 6-1 at Portland to cap their worst-to-first finish from 1995 and clinch the first of their Eastern League-record four straight championships. Every Senator makes the midnight ride home from Maine, except for one – MVP right fielder **Vladimir Guerrero** (1996), who stays behind in Portland to catch an early morning flight to join the Expos and start his Hall of Fame-worthy career in the majors.

1997: A year to the day after beating Portland for the Eastern League title, the Senators again dispatch the Sea Dogs 4-3 in the fourth and deciding game of the EL finals on fog-enveloped City Island.

2002: Infielder **Jamey Carroll** (1998-2000, 2002) makes his major league debut, starting at third base and going 2-for-3 with a walk in the Expos' 6-3 loss to the Cubs at Wrigley Field. At 28 years and 7 months, Carroll is the second-oldest position player to make his major league debut with Montreal – trailing only third baseman Coco Laboy, who was 28 years and 9 months when he starts the Expos' inaugural game in 1969.

September 12

1962: Giants outfielder **Spottswood Poles** (1906-08) dies in Harrisburg, Pa., at age 74.

1994: Binghamton's Bill Pulsipher no-hits the Senators 2-0 on City Island in Game 2 of the Eastern League finals. The closest Pulsipher comes to giving up a hit comes in the seventh inning, when he walks **Tyrone Horne** (1992-95) to start the inning, falls behind 3-1 in the count to **Tyrone Woods** (1992-94) and then uses his foot to redirect Woods' sharp grounder up the middle to shortstop Rey Ordonez, who starts a rally-killing, 1-6-4-3 double play. The Mets win the next two games in Binghamton to clinch the series.

2013: Trenton rolls to an 11-4 victory on City Island to complete a three-game sweep of the Senators in the Eastern League finals.

September 13

1898: Player-manager **Glenn Killinger** (1924, 1927-28) born in Harrisburg, Pa.

1987: The Senators beat Vermont in both ends of a day-night doubleheader on City Island for the city's first title since 1946 and the first of six EL titles over the next 13 seasons.

1993: With the Senators in Canton to complete an improbable comeback for the Eastern League title, City Island is transformed into the Cleveland Indians' spring training home for the movie "Major League 2." The island, complete with imported palm trees, is made to look like the Indians' real spring home in Winter Haven, Fla. Actors Dennis Haysbert, Charlie Sheen, Tom Berenger, Omar Epps, James Gammon and Corbin Bernsen call Harrisburg home for a couple of weeks.

1994: Using Edgardo Alfonso's two-run homer and Frank Jacobs' solo shot off the right-field scoreboard in the bottom of ninth against closer **Al Reyes** (1994), Binghamton rallies past the Senators 5-4 in Game 3 of the Eastern League finals. The Mets, winners in two of the first three games, clinch the best-of-5 series the next night.

1996: Charlie O'Brien (2000) becomes the first catcher to wear a hockey-style mask in the Blue Jays' 4-1 loss to the Yankees at Toronto's SkyDome.

September 14

1987: A day after beating Vermont for the Eastern League championship, catcher **Tom Prince** (1987), left fielder **Tommy Gregg** (1987) and shortstop **Felix Fermin** (1987) are promoted to the majors by the Pirates.

1993: USA Today names first baseman-outfielder **Cliff Floyd** (1993) as its minor league player of year after the 20-year-old Floyd bats .329 in 101 games for the Senators with 26 homers and 101 RBIs. Runners-ups include teammate **Rondell White** (1992-93, 1996), and future major league all-stars Manny Ramirez, Chipper Jones and Jim Thome.

1994: The Senators fall 7-2 at Binghamton in the fourth and deciding game of EL finals.

1999: Expos pitcher **Javier Vazquez** (1997) gives up a fourth-inning single to **Mark Grudzielanek** (1994) and nothing else in one-hitting the Dodgers 3-0 in Los Angeles.

2002: The Senators lose 5-0 at Norwich in the fifth and final game of the EL finals.

2003: Expos right fielder **Vladimir Guerrero** (1996) homers off Mets relief pitcher Dan Wheeler in his final at-bat to complete a cycle in a 7-3 victory at Olympic Stadium. Guerrero's first there hits – a double, single and triple – come off Tom Glavine.

September 15

1968: Outfielder **Marc Griffin** (1993-94) born in Quebec City, Quebec.

1993: Center fielder **Glenn Murray** (1993) drives in three runs and **Reid Cornelius** (1991-93) strikes out 10 in an 8-0 rout at Canton in the fifth and deciding game of the EL finals – a title that comes as the Senators outscore the Indians 23-4 in three road games after losing the first two at home. After the last game, the Senators purchase from Canton the 48 bottles of champagne it had been chilling since returning home with a 2-0 lead.

1997: Pitcher **Darrin Winston** (1993-94) picks up his first major league win as the Phillies' 31-year-old rookie allows one unearned run over seven innings in a 2-1 victory over the Mets in the second game of a doubleheader at Veterans Stadium.

September 16

1959: Hitting coach **Tim Raines** (2007) born in Sanford, Fla.

1964: First baseman **Herb Conyers** (1947) dies in Cleveland, Ohio, at age 43.

1982: Utility player **Michael Martinez** (2009-2010) born in Santo Domingo, D.R.

2007: Outfielder **Roger Bernadina** (2007-08) scores three runs as the Dutch national team beats Great Britain 6-1 for a berth in the 2008 Olympic Games in China.

September 17

1993: Outfielder **Curtis Pride** (1993) picks up his first hit in the majors – a pinch-hit, two-run, seventh-inning double – off Philadelphia's Bobby Thigpen before scoring the tying run in a game the Expos win 8-7 in 12 innings at Olympic Stadium.

1998: A two-run double by **Carlos Adolfo** (1998-99) in the top of the 10th inning breaks a 4-4 tie and lifts the Senators over New Britain 6-4 for the Eastern League title – tying Harrisburg with the 1984-86 Vermont Reds as the only teams in Eastern League history to win three in a row.

MILTON BRADLEY

September 18

1984: Future hitting coach **Tim Raines** (2007) steals four bases in Montreal's 7-4 victory at St. Louis to give him 70-plus steals for a major league-record fourth straight season.

September 19

1999: The Senators blow a 7-0 lead before rallying to beat Norwich 10-9 on City Island, tying the Eastern League finals 2-2 and forcing a fifth and deciding game. In addition to those 19 runs, the teams total 36 baserunners on 19 hits, 14 walks, two errors and a hit batsman in what is the wildest game in the Senators' storied playoff history. That distinction lasts only 24 hours as **Milton Bradley** (1999) ends the series the next night with a two-out, two-strike, bottom-of-ninth, straight-out-of-Hollywood grand slam.

September 20

1963: Manager **Doug Sisson** (1999-2000) born in Orlando, Fla.

1985: Shortstop **Ian Desmond** (2006, 2008-09) born in Sarasota, Fla.

1988: Infielder **Steve Lombardozzi** (2010-11) born in Fulton, Md.

1999: Center fielder **Milton Bradley** (1999) launches a two-strike, two-out grand slam to right-center off Joe Lisio in the bottom of the ninth to lift the Senators over Norwich 12-11 in the fifth and deciding game of the Eastern League finals, giving Harrisburg a league-record fourth straight title on a rainy, misty and surreal night on City Island.

2009: On the 10th anniversary of authoring the greatest single moment on City Island since the place opened for baseball in 1890, **Milton Bradley** (1999) is suspended by the Chicago Cubs for the rest of season for publicly criticizing the team.

September 21

1932: Facing a Yankees lineup with seven Hall of Famers, Philadelphia A's rookie pitcher **Sugar Cain** (1931) allows only seven hits in an 8-4 victory over New York at Shibe

Park. Three of Cain's four strikeouts come against Lou Gehrig, Tony Lazzeri and Bill Dickey. As for the great Babe Ruth, he manages only a single off Cain.

1989: The Eastern League begins its 18-day Diamond Diplomacy tour of the Soviet Union with a contingent that includes Senators manager **Dave Trembley** (1987-89), pitcher **Mouse Adams** (1988-90), catcher **Jeff Banister** (1988-90), and infielders **Tommy Shields** (1988-89) and **Kevin Burdick** (1988-89).

2000: Right fielder **Vladimir Guerrero** (1996) hits his 43rd homer – breaking his own Expos' single-season record – in a 10-3 victory over Florida at Olympic Stadium. Guerrero finishes the

SUGAR CAIN season with 44 homers. The 44 remain a franchise record until Alfonso Soriano hits 46 in 2006 – two years after the Expos relocate to Washington.

September 22

1915: Pitcher **Reese Diggs** (1935) born in Mathews, Va.

September 23

1992: Left fielder **Moises Alou** (1989-90) hits a grand slam off the Pirates' Roger Mason with one out in the bottom of the 14th to lift the Expos to a 5-1 victory in Montreal.

September 24

1964: Pitcher **Jim Neidlinger** (1987-88), who in 1987 starts the first game in the Senators' modern era, born in Vallejo, Calif.

2000: A year after leading the Senators to the Eastern League title and less than three weeks after guiding them back to the playoffs, manager **Doug Sisson** (1999-2000) is fired by the Expos for what Montreal general manager Jim Beattie calls "insubordination." Two days later, Venezuelan-born **Luis Dorante** (2001) replaces Sisson, becoming the Senators' first minority manager.

2012: Outfielder **Jimmy Van Ostrand** (2012-13) homers for the fourth time in three games as Canada tops Germany 11-1 in a World Baseball Classic qualifier in Germany.

September 25

1974: Future pitching coach **Tommy John** (2002) undergoes a revolutionary operation on his left arm, where his ulnar collateral ligament is replaced with a tendon from his right wrist. The procedure is performed by Dr. Frank Jobe and will forever be known as "Tommy John surgery." John, then with the Dodgers, returns in 1976 to pitch another 14 seasons in the majors, picking up 164 of his 288 career victories after the surgery.

September 26

1965: Pitcher **Doug Piatt** (1992) born in Beaver, Pa.

BRYCE HARPER

1969: Pitcher **Brian Looney** (1993) born in New Haven, Conn.

1979: Third baseman **Yurendell deCaster** (2008) born in Brevengat, Curacao.

2011: Baltimore DH **Vladimir Guerrero** (1996) singles off Boston's Josh Beckett in the sixth inning of a 6-3 victory at Camden Yards for his 2,586th career hit to pass Julio Franco atop the list for most hits by a Dominican-born player.

2012: Nineteen-year-old rookie outfielder **Bryce Harper** (2011, 2013) homers in the first inning off the Phillies' Kyle Kendrick in Philadelphia for his 20th of the season to join one-time Red Sox outfielder Tony Conigliaro as the only teenagers in history to hit at least 20 in a season.

September 27

1984: Pitcher **John Lannan** (2007, 2010) born in Long Beach, N.Y.

2000: Outfielder **Brad Wilkerson** (1999-2000) starts in center and **John Cotton** (2001) is the DH as Team USA upsets two-time defending champion Cuba 4-0 for the gold medal at the Olympic Games in Sydney, Australia.

2012: Infielder **Eleanor Engle** (1952) dies in Harrisburg at age 86.

September 28

1984: Third baseman **Ryan Zimmerman** (2005) born in Washington, N.C.

2011: **Stephen Strasburg** (2010-11) strikes out 10 in six shutout innings as Washington beats the Marlins 3-1 in their final home game in a football-first stadium they shared with NFL's Dolphins before moving to downtown Miami in 2012.

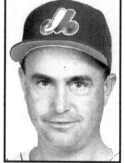

DAVE JAUSS

September 29

1977: Pitcher **Jake Westbrook** (1999) born in Athens, Ga.

1994: After telling him during the Eastern League finals that his contract would not be renewed, Expos general manager Kevin Malone formally fires Senators manager **Dave Jauss** (1994). The reason has less to do with performance – Harrisburg's 88-51 record is the Eastern League's best in 1994 – and more with finances as Jauss, the EL manager of the year, refuses to take a pay cut from $50,000 to $40,000 for 1995.

2004: Left fielder **Terrmel Sledge** (2001-02) pops up a 3-1 pitch from Rudy Seanez to third baseman Mike Mordecai for the last out of the Expos' 9-1 loss to Florida in their final game at Olympic Stadium before relocating to Washington, D.C.

September 30

1956: Outfielder **Jim Lemon** (1949) strikes out four times in the Washington Senators' 6-3 loss to Baltimore, finishing the season with a major league-record 138 strikeouts. Not that anyone remembers now as Lemon's record total from 1956 ranks only 391st on the all-time list entering the 2013 season.

1981: Outfielder **Brandon Watson** (2002-03, 2005) born in Los Angeles.

October 1

1903: Right fielder **Jimmy Sebring** (1908) hits the first home run in the first World

JIMMY SEBRING

Series game, where with one out in the seventh inning he hits an inside-the-park homer to center field off Hall of Famer Cy Young for the final run in the Pirates' 7-3 victory at Boston.

1928: Catcher **Hal Naragon** (1948-49) born in Zanesville, Ohio.

1987: Outfielder **Erik Komatsu** (2011, 2013) born in Camarillo, Calif.

1993: Baseball America names the Senators its minor league team of the year after the Senators go 94-44 in the regular season before winning another six postseason games and the Eastern League title.

2007: Infielder **Jamey Carroll** (1998-2000, 2002) lifts the Rockies into the National League playoffs when his 13th-inning sacrifice fly scores Matt Holliday, past the tag of San Diego catcher **Michael Barrett** (1998) for a 9-8 win in a 163rd, play-in game at Coors Field.

October 2

1972: Pitcher **Trey Moore** (1997) born in Houston, Tex.

2004: First baseman **Brad Wilkerson** (1999-2000) caps off the Expos' final victory before the franchise moves to Washington with a three-run homer off Braden Looper in the top of the ninth inning to beat the Mets 6-3 at Shea Stadium.

TERRMEL SLEDGE

October 3

1975: Pitcher **Mike Johnson** (1998) born in Edmonton, Alberta.

2004: A first-inning single to left by **Terrmel Sledge** (2001-02) off Tom Glavine scores **Jamey Carroll** (1998-2000, 2002) from third base to give the Expos a 1-0 lead in the franchise's final game before relocating from Montreal to Washington, D.C. The run is the Expos' only one in an 8-1 loss at Shea Stadium that comes 35 years after opening their inaugural National League season at Shea with an 11-10 victory over the Mets. Also in Montreal's final lineup are five other onetime Senators – first baseman **Brad Wilkerson** (1999-2000), shortstop **Josh Labandeira** (2003-05), center fielder **Ryan Church** (2005-06), right fielder **Valentino Pascucci** (2001-02) and pitcher **John Patterson** (2004).

October 4

2001: Future hitting coach **Tim Raines** (2007) joins his son, **Tim Raines Jr.** (2006), in the outfield during the Orioles' 5-4 loss to the Red Sox in Baltimore. The Raines' duo becomes only the second father-son combo to play in the same game, following Ken Griffey Sr. and Jr. with Seattle in 1990-91.

October 5

1954: Hall of Famer **Oscar Charleston** (1924-27) dies in Philadelphia at age 57.

1957: Shortstop **Onix Concepcion** (1987) born in Dorado, P.R.

1972: Outfielder **Yamil Benitez** (1994) born in San Juan, P.R.

1982: Pitcher **Mike Hinckley** (2004, 2007-08) born in Oklahoma City.

1999: Third baseman **Andy Tracy** (1998-99) is named the Eastern League's MVP after totaling 37 homers and 128 RBIs. He is the Senators' sixth MVP in a 10-year span.

2007: Manager **Jim Tracy** (1993) is fired after two seasons as the Pirates' manager by new general manager Neal Huntington, who as an Expos administrative assistant in the mid-1990s occasionally pitches batting practice to the Senators during his visits to City Island.

ARCHI CIANFROCCO

October 6

1893: Pitcher-manager **Johnny Tillman** (1928-30) born in Bridgeport, Conn.

1966: First baseman **Archi Cianfrocco** (1991) born in Rome, N.Y.

1983: Outfielder **Frank Diaz** (2006-07) born in Valencia, Venz.

October 7

1997: A month after leading the Senators to their second straight Eastern League title, manager **Rick Sofield** (1997) becomes Montreal's minor league field coordinator.

2012: Pinch-hitter **Tyler Moore** (2011) drives in two runs with a two-out single in the eighth inning off Marc Rzepczynski to lift the Nationals over the Cardinals 3-2 in Game 1 of the National League Division Series at Busch Stadium.

October 8

1986: Pitcher **Erik Davis** (2011-12) born in San Jose, Calif.

2010: After a $45.1 million facelift, the Senators' home on City Island is named by Baseball Digest as its Ballpark Renovation of the Year.

October 9

1963: Shortstop **Felix Fermin** (1987) born in Valverde, D.R.
1976: Outfielder **Kenny James** (1999-2001) born in Bartow, Fla.

October 10

1987: Pitcher **Danny Rosenbaum** (2011-12) born in Loveland, Ohio.

October 11

1965: Pitcher **Orlando Hernandez** (2010) born in Villa Clara, Cuba.
2012: Pitcher **Ross Detwiler** (2009-10), on the postseason roster after the Nationals shut down prized starter **Stephen Strasburg** (2010-11) a month earlier, returns to his hometown of St. Louis and holds the Cardinals to an unearned run over six innings in a 2-1 victory to tie the best-of-5 National League Division Series at two games each.

October 12

1969: First baseman **Derrick White** (1992-93) born in San Rafael, Calif.
1987: First baseman **Snake Henry** (1933) dies in Wendell, N.C., at age 92.
2012: A day after picking up the victory in Game 4 of NLDS, Washington closer **Drew Storen** (2009-10, 2012) gives up four runs in top of the ninth inning as St. Louis rallies to win 9-7 at Nationals Park. The victory moves the Cardinals into the National League Championship Series, where they lose to eventual World Series champion San Francisco.

HENRY MATEO

October 13

1903: Right fielder **Buck Freeman** (1910) leads off the fourth inning with a triple to right off Deacon Phillippe and scores three batters later on Hobe Ferris' single to center for a 1-0 lead as Boston beats Pittsburgh 3-0 in the eighth and final game of the first World Series.

October 14

1896: Hall of Fame outfielder **Oscar Charleston** (1924-27) born in Indianapolis, Ind.
1948: Pitching coach **Brent Strom** (1998) born in San Diego, Calif.
1974: Second baseman **Henry Mateo** (2000-01, 2005) born in Santo Domingo, D.R.
1978: Outfielder **Ryan Church** (2005-06) born in Santa Barbara, Calif.

October 15

1967: Shortstop **Carlos Garcia** (1989-90) born in Tachira, Venz.
1973: Pitcher **Tim Young** (1997-98) born in Gulfport, Miss.

October 16
1965: Pitcher **Ed Puig** (1993, 1995) born in Michigan City, Ind.
1992: Outfielder **Bryce Harper** (2011, 2013) born in Las Vegas, Nev.
1993: Pitcher **Jimmie DeShong** (1929-30) dies in Harrisburg, Pa., at age 83.

October 17
1965: Infielder **Charlie Montoyo** (1996) born in Florida, P.R.
1981: Pitcher **Brett Campbell** (2006-07) born in Atlanta, Ga.

October 18
1975: Infielder **Jason Camilli** (1998-2000) born in Phoenix.

October 19
1949: Backup catcher **Joe Tipton** (1946) is traded by the White Sox to the A's for Hall of Fame second baseman Nellie Fox.

JOE TIPTON

October 20
1966: Pitcher **Jonathan Hurst** (1991) born in New York City.

October 21
1993: The Sporting News selects **Jim Tracy** (1993) as its minor league manager of the year after leading the Senators to 100 victories and the Eastern League title, and names Senators general manager **Todd Vander Woude** its minor league executive of the year.

October 22
1976: Catcher **Michael Barrett** (1998) born in Atlanta, Ga.
2012: Pitcher **Bob Berresford** (1952), author of the Senators' last no-hitter in 1952 before their 35-year sabbatical, dies in Shenandoah, Pa., at age 82.

October 23
1894: Pitcher **Rube Bressler** (1913) born in Coder, Pa.
1912: Outfielder **Piggy Ward** (1893) dies in Altoona, Pa., at age 45.
1953: Pitching coach **Bo McLaughlin** (1995-96) born in Oakland, Calif.
1975: Outfielder **Jeremy Ware** (1999-2004) born in Orangeville, Ontario.
1979: Infielder **Ramon Castro** (2005) born in Carabobo, Venz.
1997: Left fielder **Moises Alou** (1989-90) hits his second three-run homer of the World Series off Cleveland's Orel Hershiser, this one helping Florida beat Cleveland 8-7 at Jacobs Field to take a 3-2 lead in a series the Marlins will win in seven games.

October 24

1911: Pitcher **Chief Bender** (1902) beats Hall of Famer Christy Mathewson and the New York Giants 4-2 at Shibe Park to give the Philadelphia Athletics a 3-1 lead in a World Series they capture two days later as Bender wins again, this time 13-2.

1961: Shortstop **Rafael Belliard** (1987) born in Pueblo Nuevo, D.R.

1967: Utility player **F.P. Santangelo** (1991) born in Livonia, Mich.

CHIEF BENDER

October 25

1967: Catcher **Joe Siddall** (1991-92) born in Windsor, Ontario.

1968: Manager **Luis Dorante** (2001) born in Falcon, Venz.

2005: In his only World Series at-bat, infielder **Geoff Blum** (1996, 1998) snaps a 5-5 tie with a solo homer in top of the 14th inning off the Houston Astros' Ezequiel Astacio to help the Chicago White Sox win 7-5 and take a commanding 3-0 lead before sweeping the series 24 hours later.

2011: First baseman **Jimmy Van Ostrand** (2012-13) accounts for both of Canada's runs with a two-run double off Andy Van Hekken in a 2-1 victory over the United States in the Pan American Games final in Guadalajara, Mexico.

October 26

1984: Catcher **Jesus Flores** (2009) born in Carupano, Venz.

October 27

1971: Pitcher **Scott Forster** (1996-99) born in Philadelphia.

1976: Infielder **Simon Pond** (1998) born in North Vancouver, British Columbia.

2007: First baseman-DH **Fernando Seguignol** (1998) drills a three-run homer in the first inning to back Yu Darvish's 13-strikeout performance as the Nippon Ham Fighters beat the Chunichi Dragons 3-1 to win the Japan Series.

October 28

1969: Pitcher **Kirk Bullinger** (1995-97) born in New Orleans, La.

2009: In the latest start for a World Series Game One, Phillies pitcher **Cliff Lee** (2002) beats the Yankees 6-1 in the Bronx. Lee also wins Game 5 in Philadelphia before the Yankees win the Series in six games.

October 29

1996: The Expos trade pitchers **Alex Pacheco** (1995-96) and Jeff Fassero to the Mariners for pitchers **Trey Moore** (1997) and Matt Wagner, and catcher Chris Widger.

October 30

1871: First baseman **Buck Freeman** (1910) born in Catasauqua, Pa.

1978: Pitcher **Reese Diggs** (1935) dies in Baltimore at age 63.

1974: Outfielder **Quincy Foster** (2002-03) born in Bronx, N.Y.

1982: Pitcher **Jonathan Albaladejo** (2007) born in San Juan, P.R.

1997: The Expos name former major league catcher and coach **Rick Sweet** (1998-99) as the Senators' manager, replacing **Rick Sofield** (1997).

1999: The "Clown Prince of Baseball," **Max Patkin**, whose 50-year career of spoofing and goofing begins on City Island in 1948, dies in Paoli, Pa., at age 79.

October 31

1951: Manager **Dave Trembley** (1987-90) born in Carthage, N.Y.

1969: First baseman **Oreste Marrero** (1993) born in Bayamon, P.R.

1973: Future pitching coach **Jerry Reuss** (2000) is traded by the Houston Astros to the Pittsburgh Pirates for catcher Milt May.

November 1

1989: Future managers **Jim Tracy** (1993), **Pat Kelly** (1995-96) and **Keith Bodie** (2005) are among the retired major leaguers dusted off as the Senior Professional Baseball Association begins its first and only full season in Florida.

2000: The Dodgers name **Jim Tracy** (1993) as their manager, replacing Davey Johnson.

2011: Reds second baseman **Brandon Phillips** (2001-02) wins his second straight – and third overall – National League Gold Glove.

November 2

1966: First baseman-outfielder **Orlando Merced** (1989) born in Hato Rey, P.R.

1970: Outfielder **Tyrone Horne** (1992-95) born in Troy, N.C.

1974: Shortstop **Orlando Cabrera** (1997) born in Cartagena, Columbia.

1987: Harrisburg mayor **Stephen Reed** announces the Senators turn a $30,000 profit in their first season back on City Island.

1990: Center fielder **Brian Goodwin** (2012-13) born in Rocky Mount, N.C.

2011: The Cubs fire manager **Mike Quade** (1991-92) after a season-plus running team.

BRIAN GOODWIN

November 3

2009: After six seasons in Anaheim, outfielder-DH **Vladimir Guerrero** (1996) is out of work – albeit briefly – after the Angels decline the option on his contract for 2010. Guerrero eventually signs with Texas and helps the Rangers reach the 2010 World Series.

November 4

1948: Outfielder **Jake Powell** (1933) grabs a gun in a Washington, D.C, police station and fatally shoots himself. He is 40.

1971: Pitcher **Melvin Bunch** (1997) born in Texarkana, Tex.

1993: The Expos name **Dave Jauss** (1994) as the Senators' manager, replacing Class AAA-bound **Jim Tracy** (1993).

2002: Expos outfielder **Brad Wilkerson** (1999-2000) finishes second to Colorado pitcher Jason Jennings in the voting for National League Rookie of the Year.

November 5

1978: Pitcher **Corey Thurman** (2004) born in Augusta, Ga.

1987: The Eastern League names **Rick Redd** (1987-92) its general manager of the year.

November 6

1899: Outfielder **Joe Munson** (1925) born in Renovo, Pa.

1975: Pitcher **Brandon Agamennone** (1999-2002) born in Washington, D.C.

1983: Outfielder **Justin Maxwell** (2008) born in Olney, Md.

1984: Pitcher **Atahualpa Severino** (2009) born in Cotui, D.R.

1987: Harrisburg is named the host city for the 1988 Eastern League All-Star Game.

November 7

1966: Pitcher **Rube Bressler** (1913) dies in Mount Washington, Ohio, at age 72.

1967: Pitcher **David Wainhouse** (1991) born in Toronto.

November 8

1958: Pitcher **Paul Wilmet** (1987-88) born in Green Bay, Wis.

2012: Nationals shortstop **Ian Desmond** (2006, 2008-09) and pitcher **Stephen Strasburg** (2010-11) earn National League Silver Slugger Awards for being the best hitters at their position.

November 9

1973: Future pitching coach **Dave Tomlin** (1994) is traded with outfielder Bobby Tolan from the Reds to the Padres for pitcher Clay Kirby.

1977: Outfielder **Peter Bergeron** (1998-99) born in Greenfield, Mass.

1981: Pitcher **Chuck James** (2010) born in Atlanta, Ga.

1987: Baseball America names **Dave Trembley** (1987-89) its minor league manager of the year.

1992: Career minor league pitcher **Travis Buckley** (1992) becomes the first player acquired in a trade by the expansion Colorado Rockies in a deal that sends pitcher Matt Connolly, another minor league lifer, to the Expos.

November 10

1974: Pitcher **Micah Bowie** (2005) born in Humble, Tex.

1977: Outfielder **Matt Cepicky** (2001-02) born in St. Louis, Mo.

1983: Pitcher **Ryan Mattheus** (2011-13) born in Galt, Calif.

2007: Outfielder **Brett Roneberg** (2002) goes from position player to pitcher and records the final three outs for Australia in a 26-1 caning of Thailand at the Baseball World Cup tournament in Taiwan.

BRETT RONEBERG

November 11

1892: Pitcher **Al Schacht** (1915) born in New York City.

1998: The Expos name **Doug Sisson** (1999-2000) as the Senators' manager, replacing **Rick Sweet** (1998-99).

2010: In his first and only season with the Rangers, **Vladimir Guerrero** (1996) earns his final Silver Slugger Award – and eighth overall – as the American League's best designated hitter.

November 12

1968: Manager **Randy Knorr** (2010) born in San Gabriel, Calif.

1973: Pitcher **J.D. Smart** (1997-98) born in San Saba, Tex.

1996: The Expos name **Rick Sofield** (1997) as the Senators' manager six days after promoting **Pat Kelly** (1995-96) to Class AAA Ottawa.

2012: Outfielder **Bryce Harper** (2011, 2013) is named the National League Rookie of the Year. The 19-year-old Harper is the youngest position player to win the award in the league.

November 13

1965: Catcher **Bob Natal** (1991) born in Long Beach, Calif.

2008: Cliff Lee (2002) wins the American League Cy Young Award after going 22-3 with a 2.54 ERA for Cleveland.

BOB NATAL

November 14

2005: After winning the award in 2004, Angels designated hitter **Vladimir Guerrero** (1996) finishes third in the American League MVP balloting behind Yankees third baseman Alex Rodriguez and Red Sox DH David Ortiz.

November 15

1949: Manager **Marc Bombard** (1990) born in Baltimore.

2007: Popular general manager **Todd Vander Woude**, a front-office fixture since the Senators' return in 1987, resigns. Vander Woude, a two-time Eastern League executive of the year is replaced 12 days later by longtime local television advertising executive **Randy Whitaker**.

2010: Infielder **Geoff Blum** (1996, 1998) signs a two-year, $2.7 million contract with Arizona.

November 16

1968: Pitcher **Chris Haney** (1991) born in Baltimore.

RANDY WHITAKER

1978: Pitcher **Kip Bouknight** (2005-06) born in Columbia, S.C.

2004: Vladimir Guerrero (1996) is named the American League MVP after batting .337 with 39 homers and 126 RBIs as Anaheim's designated hitter.

November 17

1978: Outfielder **Valentino Pascucci** (2001-02) born in Bellflower, Calif.

1992: The Florida Marlins and Colorado Rockies select three former Senators in the expansion draft with catcher **Bob Natal** (1991) and pitcher **Richie Lewis** (1991) going to Florida and pitcher **Doug Bochtler** (1992) heading to Colorado.

2004: Manager **Marc Bombard** (1990) becomes the Philadelphia Phillies' first-base coach.

2011: Catcher **Brian Schneider** (1999) signs his final contract, a one-year deal worth $800,000 with the Phillies before retiring after the 2012 season.

2011: Manager **Randy Knorr** (2010) is named the Nationals' bench coach.

JAKE WESTBROOK

November 18

1884: Pitcher **Rip Vowinkel** (1912) born in Oswego, N.Y.

1892: Manager **Les Mann** (1934) born in Lincoln, Neb.

1997: The Expos trade infielder **Mike Lansing** (1992) to the Colorado Rockies for pitchers **Jake Westbrook** (1999) and John Nicholson, and outfielder Mark Hamlin.

2009: Manager **Jim Tracy** (1993) is named the National League's manager of the year after replacing the fired Clint Hurdle and leading the Rockies to a 74-42 finish, and into the playoffs.

November 19

1970: First baseman **J.J. Thobe** (1994) born in Covington, Ky.

1978: First baseman **Jeff Bailey** (2002-03) born in Longview, Wash.

2007: The Angels trade shortstop **Orlando Cabrera** (1997) to the White Sox for pitcher Jon Garland.

2008: The Nationals rehire **John Stearns** (2006, 2008-09) for a third season as the Senators' manager. The Nationals also name onetime Senator **Randy Tomlin** (1989-90) as Stearns' pitching coach for 2009.

November 20

1971: Pitcher **Gabe White** (1993) born in Sebring, Fla.

November 21

2011: The Phillies hire corner infielder and 1999 EL MVP **Andy Tracy** (1998-99) to manage their short-season, Class A team in Williamsport, where Tracy stays for one season before becoming the organization's minor league hitting coordinator.

GABE WHITE

November 22

1984: First baseman-outfielder **Bill Rhinehart** (2008-11) born in Roseville, Calif.

1993: The Eastern League OKs **Van Farber** as the Senators' new owner, but the move is rejected five months later by the National Association of Professional Baseball Leagues, which questions Farber's finances.

November 23

1963: Pitcher **Rich Sauveur** (1987) born in Arlington, Va.

1970: Outfielder **Glenn Murray** (1993) born in Manning, S.C.

November 24

1984: Infielder **Joel Guzman** (2009) born in San Pedro de Macoris, D.R.

2004: After four straight winning seasons, the Dodgers give a two-year contract extension to manager **Jim Tracy** (1993).

2005: Pitcher **Guillermo Mota** (1998) joins pitcher Josh Beckett and third baseman Mike Lowell in a trade that sends them from the Florida Marlins to the Boston Red Sox for four prospects, including shortstop Hanley Ramirez and Anibal Sanchez.

November 25

1971: Pitcher **Tavo Alvarez** (1992, 1995) born in Sonora, Mexico.

1987: Pitcher **Nate Karns** (2013) born in Franklin, Pa.

November 26
1976: Catcher **Brian Schneider** (1999) born in Jacksonville, Fla.

November 27
1969: Catcher **Tim Laker** (1991-92) born in Encino, Calif.

November 28
1973: Shortstop **Edgar Tovar** (1993, 1995) born in Aragua, Venz.

2010: Pitcher **Javier Vazquez** (1997) signs a one-year, $7 million contract with the Marlins, his fourth team since 2008.

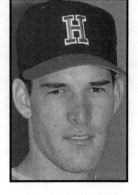

TIM LAKER

November 29
2011: *Baseball America* selects the Senators for its annual Bob Freitas Award as the top Class AA team.

November 30
1909: Pitcher **Jimmie DeShong** (1929-30) born in Harrisburg, Pa.

1968: Pitcher **Heath Haynes** (1992-93) born in Wheeling, W.Va.

1993: The Senators receive the annual Bob Freitas Award by *Baseball America* as the best-run Class AA team, capping a season in which they win 100 games and the EL title.

December 1
1970: Pitcher **Kirk Rueter** (1993) born in Hoyleton, Ill.

1975: Hall of Fame second baseman **Nellie Fox** of St. Thomas, Pa., dies in Baltimore at age 47.

2011: The Nationals name onetime Minnesota Twins and Washington catcher **Matt LeCroy** (2012-13) as the Senators' new manager, replacing the Class AAA-bound **Tony Beasley** (2011). The Nationals also assign two other former major leaguers to LeCroy's staff – pitching coach **Paul Menhart** (2012-13) and past hitting coach **Eric Fox** (2001, 2012-13).

JAVIER VAZQUEZ

December 2
1971: Future pitching coach **Tommy John** (2002) is traded from the Chicago White Sox to the Los Angeles Dodgers for first baseman Dick Allen.

December 3

1964: Outfielder **Steve Carter** (1988) born in Charlottesville, Va.

1974: Future National League All-Star catcher and Senators manager **John Stearns** (2006, 2008-09), then among the Philadelphia Phillies' top prospects, is traded with outfielder Del Unser and pitcher Mac Scarce to the New York Mets for closer Tug McGraw, and outfielders Don Hahn and Dave Schneck.

1981: Harrisburg Giants infielder **Rev Cannady** (1925-27) dies in Fort Myers, Fla., at age 79.

December 4

1890: Pitcher **Bob Shawkey** (1911) born in Sigel, Pa.

1981: Pitcher **Jerome Williams** (2007) born in Honolulu.

2002: The Dodgers trade shortstop **Mark Grudzielanek** (1994) and first baseman Eric Karros to the Cubs for catcher Todd Hundley and outfielder Chad Hermansen.

2008: The White Sox deal pitchers **Javier Vazquez** (1997) and Boone Logan to the Braves for utility player Brent Lillibridge and three prospects, including catcher Tyler Flowers.

December 5

1966: Manager **Tony Beasley** (2011) born in Fredericksburg, Va.

1972: First baseman-outfielder **Cliff Floyd** (1993) born in Chicago.

1983: Outfielder **Chris Rahl** (2011-12) born in Morristown, N.J.

1989: The Pirates name onetime minor league pitcher **Marc Bombard** (1990) as the Senators' manager, replacing **Dave Trembley** (1987-89).

JEFF KOBERNUS

December 6

1954: Pitching coach **Mike Parrott** (1992) born in Oxnard, Calif.

1968: Harrisburg Giants outfielder **Fats Jenkins** (1924-27) dies in Philadelphia at 70.

1972: Pitcher **Neil Weber** (1995-97) born in Newport Beach, Calif.

2012: Pitcher **Danny Rosenbaum** (2011-12) and second baseman **Jeff Kobernus** (2012) are selected by Colorado and Detroit in the Rule V draft. They rejoin the Nationals in March 2013 for $25,000 each – half of what the Rockies and Tigers paid to draft them.

December 7

1914: After 12 seasons with the A's, Hall of Fame pitcher **Chief Bender** (1902) signs with the upstart Federal League, where he plays one season for Baltimore.

1977: Pitcher **Saul Rivera** (2002, 2004-05) born in San Juan, P.R.

December 8

1947: The Pirates trade shortstop **Billy Cox** (1940-41), pitcher Preacher Roe and infielder Gene Mauch to the Dodgers for pitchers Vic Lombardi and Hal Gregg, and former National League batting champion Dixie Walker.

1972: Infielder **Jolbert Cabrera** (1994-97) born in Cartagena, Columbia.

1981: Infielder-outfielder **Kory Casto** (2006) born in Salem, Ore.

2005: The Nationals trade outfielder **Brad Wilkerson** (1999-2000), first baseman-outfielder **Terrmel Sledge** (2001-02) and pitcher **Armando Galarraga** (2005) to the Rangers for All-Star second baseman Alfonso Soriano.

December 9

1965: Pitcher **Joe Ausanio** (1990, 1993) born in Kingston, N.Y.

1986: The Eastern League approves the relocation of the Nashua franchise owned by **Jerry Mileur** from New Hampshire to Harrisburg.

2007: Outfielder **Milton Bradley** (1999) signs a one-year, $5 million deal with Texas.

2010: The Phillies select infielder **Michael Martinez** (2009-10) in the Rule V draft.

2011: The Nationals trade pitcher **Collin Balester** (2006-07) to the Tigers for pitcher **Ryan Perry** (2012-13).

December 10

1978: Pitcher **Donnie Bridges** (2000-02, 2004-05) born in Hattiesburg, Miss.

2010: Former Pirates and Nationals coach **Tony Beasley** (2011) becomes the Senators' manager after the Nationals promote manager **Randy Knorr** (2010) to AAA Syracuse.

December 11

1973: Infielder **Andy Tracy** (1998-99) born in Bowling Green, Ohio.

2006: Onetime Senators outfielder **Scott Little** (1988) is named the Senators' manager, replacing **John Stearns** (2006, 2008-09). The Nationals also hire former Expos All-Star outfielder **Tim Raines** as Little's hitting coach for 2007.

MIGUEL BATISTA

December 12

1996: Outfielder **Moises Alou** (1989-90) OKs a five-year, $25 million deal with Florida.

1997: The Expos trade pitcher **Miguel Batista** (1993-94) to the Cubs for outfielder Henry Rodriguez.

2007: Former manager **Dave Huppert** (2002) is named the first manager of the Lehigh Valley Iron Pigs, the Philadelphia Phillies' Class AAA affiliate.

December 13

1954: Seven years after acquiring the pair from Pittsburgh, Brooklyn trades infielder **Billy Cox** (1940-41) and pitcher Preacher Roe to the Baltimore Orioles for two minor leaguers and $50,000.

1975: Manager **Matt LeCroy** (2012-13) born in Belton, S.C.

1981: Infielder **Vince Rooi** (2004-05) born in Amsterdam, Netherlands.

1996: In a record-setting trade involving players with first names starting with the letter "J" – and specifically those named Jeff – the Pittsburgh Pirates send third baseman **Jeff King** (1987-88) and shortstop Jay Bell to the Royals for third baseman Joe Randa, pitchers Jeff Granger, Jeff Martin and Jeff Wallace.

2007: Former Senators infielder **F.P. Santangelo** (1991), catcher **Tim Laker** (1991-92), shortstop **Mike Lansing** (1992) and center fielder **Rondell White** (1992-93, 1996) are among 89 players the Mitchell Report cites for using performance-enhancing drugs.

December 14

1901: Player-manager **Les Bell** (1933, 1940-41, 1946-51) born in Harrisburg, Pa.

December 15

1940: Player-manager and Hall of Fame outfielder **Billy Hamilton** (1905-06) dies in Worcester, Mass., at age 74.

1992: The Expos hire former Cubs outfielder **Jim Tracy** (1993) as the Senators' next manager to replace Class AAA-bound **Mike Quade** (1991-92).

BILLY HAMILTON

2010: Almost a year to the day after he is traded from Philadelphia to Seattle for pitchers Phillippe Aumont and J.C. Ramirez, as well as outfielder Tyson Gilles, pitcher **Cliff Lee** (2002) returns to the Phillies as a free agent, signing a five-year deal worth $107.5 million.

December 16

1922: The Eastern Colored League organizes to begin play in 1923 with the Harrisburg Giants quickly becoming one of the league's best teams during their stay from 1923-27.

1938: The Boston Bees trade catcher **Ray Mueller** (1932-34) to Pittsburgh for catcher Al Todd and outfielder Johnny Dickshot.

1956: Manager **Rick Sofield** (1997) born in Cheyenne, Wyo.

1994: The Expos name onetime Toronto catcher **Pat Kelly** (1995-96) to replace **Dave Jauss** (1994) as the Senators' manager. Former All-Star second baseman Tom Herr and two ex-major league catchers – Tim Blackwell and Bill Plummer – also are finalists for the job.

JAMEY CARROLL

2009: Infielder **Jamey Carroll** (1998-2000, 2002) signs a two-year, $3.8 million contract with the Dodgers.

December 17

1965: Outfielder **Jeff Cook** (1987-90) born in Kansas City, Mo.

1968: Outfielder **Curtis Pride** (1993) born in Washington, D.C.

1976: First baseman-outfielder **Jon Tucker** (1998-99) born in Granada Hills, Calif.

1980: First baseman **Larry Broadway** (2003-05) born in Miami, Fla.

2001: Outfielder **Rondell White** (1992-93, 1996) signs a two-year, $10 million contract with the Yankees, who trade him after one season to the Padres.

2007: After the Senators' dismal 55-86 finish, the Nationals bring back manager **John Stearns** (2006, 2008-09) to replace **Scott Little** (2007).

December 18

2001: The Reds trade pitchers **Gabe White** (1993) and Luke Hudson to the Rockies for second baseman Pokey Reese and pitcher Dennys Reyes.

2009: The Cubs send underachieving outfielder **Milton Bradley** (1999) to Seattle for equally underwhelming pitcher Carlos Silva.

December 19

1971: Pitcher **Ruben Niebla** (1998-99) born in Calexico, Calif.

2000: Pitcher **Lou Polli** (1927) dies in Berlin, Vt., at age 99.

2001: Outfielder **Moises Alou** (1989-90) signs a three-year, $27 million deal with the Cubs.

FELIX FERMIN

December 20

1990: After four seasons with the Pirates, the Senators begin looking for a new major league affiliate. The Senators eventually align themselves with the Montreal Expos, a move that sets up Harrisburg to become the minors' most dominant team for the rest of the millennium.

1993: The Indians trade shortstop **Felix Fermin** (1987) and first baseman Reggie Jefferson to Seattle for shortstop Omar Vizquel.

2002: After splitting a dizzying season between the Marlins, Expos and Red Sox, first baseman-outfielder **Cliff Floyd** (1993) rejects salary arbitration from Boston and eventually signs a four-year, $26 million contract with the Mets.

December 21

1995: Pitcher **Aaron Dorlarque** (1996) accompanies former All-Star first baseman Wally Joyner on his trade from Kansas City to San Diego for second baseman Bip Roberts and pitcher Bryan Wolff.

December 22:

1909: Outfielder **Jimmy Sebring** (1908) dies in Williamsport at age 27.

1999: The Expos trade pitchers **Jake Westbrook** (1999), **Christian Parker** (1998-99) and Ted Lilly to the Yankees for pitcher Hideki Irabu.

2005: Changing teams for the fifth time in five years, outfielder **Rondell White** (1992-93, 1996) signs a two-year, $5 million contract with the Twins.

2006: Harrisburg mayor **Stephen Reed** says he has 17 bidders interested in purchasing the city-owned Senators and announces a deal will be made in 2007.

2009: The Braves trade pitchers **Javier Vazquez** (1997) and Boone Logan to the Yankees for outfielder Melky Cabrera, and pitchers Michael Dunn and Arodys Vizcaino.

2011: The Nationals send pitchers **Tommy Milone** (2010), **Brad Peacock** (2010-11) and **A.J. Cole** (2013), as well as catcher **Derek Norris** (2011), to the Oakland A's for All-Star pitcher Gio Gonzalez and minor league pitcher **Robert Gilliam** (2012-13). The Nationals reacquire Cole 13 months later, along with pitchers **Ian Krol** (2013) and **Blake Treinen** (2013), in a three-team trade that sends Washington outfielder **Michael Morse** (2012) to Seattle with the Mariners then shipping catcher John Jaso to Oakland.

HINKEY HAINES

December 23

1898: Outfielder **Hinkey Haines** (1933) born in Red Lion, Pa.

2002: Texas signs pitcher **Ugueth Urbina** (1993-94) to a one-year, $4.5 million deal.

December 24

1992: The Dodgers trade shortstop **Tim Barker** (1993) to the Expos for infielder Tim Wallach.

December 25

1927: Hall of Fame second baseman **Nellie Fox** born in St. Thomas, Pa.

December 26

1964: Third baseman **Jeff King** (1987-88) is born in Marion, Ind.

1976: Third baseman **Scott Hodges** (2000-02, 2005) born in Louisville, Ky.

1985: Former major leaguer and player-manager **Les Bell** (1933, 1940-41, 1946-51) dies in Hershey, Pa., at age 84.

December 27

1887: Giants outfielder **Spottswood Poles** (1906-08) born in Winchester, Va.

1932: Catcher **Pop Schriver** (1906-07) dies in New York City at age 67.

1986: The Pirates name **Dave Trembley** (1986-89) as the first manager in the Senators' modern era.

December 28

1937: Longtime sports announcer and Phillies broadcaster **Andy Musser**, a batboy with the Senators in the early 1950s, born in Harrisburg, Pa.

1994: Major League Baseball approves the sale of the Senators for $4.1 million from **Jerry Mileur** to four investors from suburban Philadelphia – a group that includes Reading Phillies owner Craig Stein. Within hours, reports begin to circulate from the Lehigh Valley that officials there are trying to lure the Senators to move into a proposed $10 million stadium near Easton.

Harrisburg native Andy Musser, foreground, goes from local bat boy to nationally known sportscaster. He is pictured here in the press box at Philadelphia's Connie Mack Stadium with Phillies legendary announcers Gene Kelly, center, and By Saam in 1956, when the 18-year-old Musser wins a regional contest for budding broadcasters.

December 29

1981: Infielder **Marcos Yepez** (2006-08) born in Caracas, Venz.

December 30

1962: Shortstop **Joe Boley** (1917) dies in Mahanoy City, Pa., at age 66.

1967: Pitcher **Archie Corbin** (1993) born in Beaumont, Tex.

1976: Pitcher **Chuck Crumpton** (2000-04) born in Temple, Tex.

December 31

1955: Manager **Jim Tracy** (1993) born in Hamilton, Ohio.

1980: Pitcher **Bob Shawkey** (1911) dies in Syracuse, N.Y., at age 90.

Advertising sign, measuring 6 feet by 18 inches, from Island Park in the early 1950s

References

PUBLICATIONS and WEBSITES

Baseball Almanac (www.baseball-almanac.com)
Baseball Reference (www.baseball-reference.com)
Dauphin County Library System (www.dcls.org)
Major League Baseball (www.mlb.com)
Minor League Baseball (www.milb.com)
PennLive (www.pennlive.com)
Harrisburg Patriot and Evening News, editions 1986-2013

PHOTOGRAPHS

Every effort was made to determine the ownership of the photographs in this book, and to receive permission from the copyright holders:

Senators signing autographs, author's collection; Gabe White, courtesy of Harrisburg Senators; Doug Piatt, author's collection; Jim Tracy's Topps contract, author's collection; Joey Eischen, Harrisburg Senators; Curtis Pride, author's collection; Jerry Reuss headshot, Harrisburg Senators; Hassan Pena headshot, Harrisburg Senators; 1996 Eastern League championship celebration, Harrisburg Senators; Eastern League championship ring, Harrisburg Senators; Dave Trembley during infield practice, Harrisburg Senators; Tony Longmire headshot, Harrisburg Senators; Scott Ruskin headshot, Harrisburg Senators; Chris Andre, photo by author; Bob Henley headshot, Harrisburg Senators; Peter Bergeron headshot, Harrisburg Senators; Doug Sisson and Milton Bradley, Harrisburg Senators, photo by Steve Eddy; Matt LeCroy, photo by Kyle Mace; Bo McLaughlin headshot, unknown; RiverSide Stadium photo, unknown; Metro Bank Stadium photo, Harrisburg Senators; Island Park illustration, author's collection; City Island photo, unknown; Island Park 1936 flood, author's collection; Island Park, unknown; City Island 1972 flood, unknown; RiverSide Stadium batting practice, Harrisburg Senators; Island Park illustration, author's collection; RiverSide Stadium rendering, Harrisburg Senators; City Island construction photo, Harrisburg Senators; RiverSide Stadium, 1987; Harrisburg Senators; Rob Russell in bullpen, Harrisburg Senators; Metro Bank Park, author's photo; Cliff Floyd headshot, Harrisburg Senators; Tony Armas Jr. headshot, Senators; Tony Armas Sr. headshot, unknown; F.P. Santangelo headshot, Senators; Talmadge Nunnari, Senators; Jamey Carroll, Senators; 1987 clubhouse, Senators; Danny Rueckel headshot, Senators; City Island 2011 flood, photo courtesy of Tim Foreman; RiverSide Stadium 1997 flood, author's collection; Tim Foreman, photo by author; Kirk Bullinger headshot, Harrisburg Senators;

When City Island reopens for baseball in 1987, newspaper and television photographers routinely would position themselves atop the first-base dugout. Here, they take their spots during the 1987 finals against Vermont.

Billy Cox headshot, unknown; Brian Schneider, Harrisburg Senators (Steven Eddy); Neil Weber headshot, Harrisburg Senators; Randy Tomlin 1990 photo, Harrisburg Senators; Stephen Strasburg, photo by Will Bentzel; Senators 1993 trophy photo, Harrisburg Senators; 1993 Eastern League finals Game 5 lineup card, author's collection; Bryan Hebson headshot, unknown; Cliff Floyd batting, Harrisburg Senators; Ed Bady headshot, unknown; Frank Cacciatore headshot, Harrisburg Senators; Mike Quade headshot, Harrisburg Senators; Jimmie DeShong, unknown; Joey Eischen headshot, Harrisburg Senators; Chris Stowers headshot, Harrisburg Senators; Vladimir Guerrero in dugout, Harrisburg Senators; Dave Trembley clinic, Harrisburg Senators; Kevin Burdick headshot, Harrisburg Senators; Cliff Floyd pickoff, Harrisburg Senators; Jeff Banister headshot, Harrisburg Senators; Brent Strom headshot, unknown; John Stearns headshot, Harrisburg Senators; Todd Vander Woude headshot, Harrisburg Senators; Dave Trembley and Dave Machemer, Harrisburg Senators; Tommy Gregg, unknown; Brian Schneider, Harrisburg Senators; Rap Dixon headshot, unknown; Mike Quade, Harrisburg Senators; Rob Ducey headshot, Harrisburg Senators; Senators dugout, Harrisburg Senators; Vladimir Gorilla bobblehead, unknown; F.P. Santangelo fielding, Harrisburg Senators; Pat Kelly headshot, Harrisburg Senators; Senators in Reading clubhouse, photo courtesy of Bryan Hebson; Rick Redd and Scott Carter, Harrisburg Senators; Anthony Ferrari headshot, Harrisburg Senators; Shayne Bennett headshot, Harrisburg Senators; Player lineup for national anthem, Harrisburg Senators; Marc Bombard, Harrisburg Senators; Rich Sauveur and Tom Prince, Harrisburg Senators; Doug Harris, Harrisburg Senators (Will Bentzel); Vladimir Guerrero, photo by Steven Eddy, Harrisburg Senators; 1997 Eastern League championship celebration, Harrisburg Senators; 1991 Eastern League championship celebration, Harrisburg Senators; Brandon

CLIPPINGS

Watson, Harrisburg Senators; Milton Bradley, photo by Steven Eddy; Eleanor Engle, courtesy of Eleanor Engle; Moises Alou headshot, Harrisburg Senators; Josh Johnson headshot, Harrisburg Senators; Brad Fullmer headshot, Harrisburg Senators; Rick Sweet headshot, unknown; Tyler Moore headshot, Harrisburg Senators; Chief Meyers headshot, unknown, Joe Caffie headshot, unknown; Rondell White headshot, Harrisburg Senators; Harry O'Neill headshot, unknown; Sandy Leon headshot, Harrisburg Senators; Brett Gideon headshot, Harrisburg Senators; Shane Andrews headshot, Harrisburg Senators; Mike Lansing headshot, Harrisburg Senators; Brad Wilkerson headshot, Harrisburg Senators; Edgar Tovar headshot, Harrisburg Senators; Crash Brown headshot, Harrisburg Senators; Brian Schneider headshot, Harrisburg Senators; Dave Huppert headshot, unknown; Mike Hardge headshot, Harrisburg Senators; Valentino Pascucci headshot, Harrisburg Senators; Troy Mattes headshot, unknown; Seung Song headshot, Harrisburg Senators; Greg Fulton headshot, Harrisburg Senators; Paul Denny headshot, Harrisburg Senators; Ian Krol headshot, Harrisburg Senators; Doggie Miller headshot, unknown; Al Reyes headshot, Harrisburg Senators; Jeff King headshot, Harrisburg Senators; Ben Abner headshot, Harrisburg Senators; Nate Karns headshot, Harrisburg Senators; Jim Lemon headshot, unknown; Bill Dietrich headshot, unknown; Rick Sofield headshot, Harrisburg Senators; Guillermo Mota headshot, Harrisburg Senators; Gene Moore headshot, unknown; Dave Trembley headshot, Harrisburg Senators; Dan DeMent headshot, Harrisburg Senators; Dave Machemer headshot, unknown; Eddie Onslow headshot, unknown; Buck Freeman headshot, unknown; Willis headshot, unknown; Bryce Harper program, photo by Will Bentzel; Max Patkin, author's collection; Pop Schriver, unknown; Ugueth Urbina headshot, Harrisburg Senators; Al Schacht headshot, unknown; Jim Tracy headshot, Harrisburg Senators; Joe Boley headshot, unknown; Brooks Lawrence, author's collection; Glenn Killinger, unknown; Matt LeCroy headshot, unknown; Orlando Cabrera headshot, Harrisburg Senators; Brandon Phillips headshot, Harrisburg Senators; Hiram Bocachica headshot, Harrisburg Senators; Geoff Blum headshot, Harrisburg Senators; Chris Haney headshot, Harrisburg Senators; Shawn Hill headshot, Harrisburg Senators; Fats Jenkins headshot, unknown; Andy Tracy headshot, author's collection; Matt Stairs headshot, Harrisburg Senators; Willie Mays headshot, unknown; Donnie Bridges headshot, Harrisburg Senators; Tommy Shields headshot, Harrisburg Senators; Joe Siddall headshot, Harrisburg Senators; Joe Ausanio headshot, Harrisburg Senators; Tyrone Woods headshot, Harrisburg Senators; Milton Bradley headshot, Harrisburg Senators; Sugar Cain headshot, unknown; Bryce Harper headshot, Harrisburg Senators; Dave Jauss headshot, Montreal Expos; Jimmy Sebring headshot, unknown; Terrmel Sledge headshot, Harrisburg Senators; Archi Cianfrocco, Harrisburg Senators; Henry Mateo headshot, Harrisburg Senators; Joe Tipton headshot, unknown; Chief Bender headshot, unknown; Brian Goodwin headshot, Harrisburg Senators; Brett Roneberg, unknown; Bob Natal headshot, Harrisburg Senators; Randy Whitaker headshot, Harrisburg Senators; Jake Westbrook headshot, Harrisburg Senators; Gabe White headshot, Harrisburg Senators; Tim Laker headshot, Harrisburg Senators; Javier Vazquez headshot, Harrisburg Senators; Jeff Kobernus headshot, Harrisburg Senators; Miguel Batista headshot, Harrisburg Senators; Billy Hamilton headshot, unknown; Jamey Carroll headshot, author's collection; Felix Fermin headshot, Harrisburg Senators; Hinkey Haines, unknown; Andy Musser, author's collection; 1950s Senators advertising sign, author's collection; photographers on dugout photo, Harrisburg Senators.

Index

Acknowledgments

The initial question came only days after the release of *One Patch of Grass* in May 2012, and it came independently from three people who already had finished reading my first book.

"When's the next one coming out?"

To this day, I am not sure if these people were serious, but I do remember thinking at the time that a second book certainly would be a great outlet for the 1,829 – give or take a couple of dozen – other cool things I couldn't fit into the first book. A second book also meant that I might be able to put off that five-page, single-spaced, honey-do list I had promised to complete for my wife after the first book.

But, dear, the public demands another book!

Ergo, the idea of *Clippings* was conceived.

Along the way, other folks who had read *One Patch of Grass* also asked about a sequel and, equally important, asked how they could reserve a copy.

So there, you have only yourselves to blame for this book.

Of course, a book of this nature never would have been possible without the players, managers and coaches who created the moments and then, good or bad, were left to describe them. They get the biggest thanks; otherwise, you end up with a lot of empty pages here.

The bulk of the research for this book was done through personal archives (i.e. those 47 Hammermill paper boxes taking up residence in the family room) and the archives of The Patriot-News, where the aforementioned moments and thoughts were captured for posterity by the beat writers – Skip Hutter, Geoff Morrow and, well, me – who covered the overwhelming majority of the Harrisburg Senators' games from their return to City Island in 1987 through the 2013 season.

Many thanks, too, to Senators general manager Randy Whitaker for allowing me to once again tap into the team's photo archives.

Priceless stuff.

As he did for *One Patch of Grass*, computer savant Bill Kratzer – the webmaster for www.harrisburgbaseball.com – kept alive my laptop for this project. Bill also taught me the secrets of the "Control Z" key, as well as how to dropkick a printer.

As always, my thanks to Michelle Linker, my bride since the end of the last millennium who possesses both the innate skills of a first-rate, front-line newspaper copy editor and infinite patience with the process.

Finally, I am forever grateful to our daughter, Annie, aka the Little General, who during the course of this project learned how to throw both a four-seam and two-seam fastball with equal aplomb – no small feat for a 9 year old.

She always had the good sense and great timing to pull me away from the laptop and remind me that having a catch with her in the backyard can be much more fun than writing about catches made by others at the ballpark.

ABOUT THE AUTHOR

Andrew Linker is an award-winning sports writer who has spent more than 30 years working for newspapers and magazines up and down the Susquehanna River. Most of that time has been spent covering the Harrisburg Senators since their return to City Island in 1987. He and his wife Michelle and their daughter Annie live in Palmyra, Pa. – exactly 19.8 miles from home plate on City Island. His first book, *One Patch of Grass*, was published in May 2012.

Made in the USA
Columbia, SC
16 May 2018